WATER SKIING

D1411977

by Al Tyll

**National Champion
1962-63-64-65**

**Seven Times
World's Record Holder**

arco
New York

Published by ARCO PUBLISHING COMPANY, Inc.
219 Park Avenue South, New York, N.Y. 10003

Library of Congress Catalog Card Number 67-10475

Arco Catalog Number 1519

Printed in the United States of America

DEDICATION

The best of all—the greatest thing water skiing did for me, was to bring to me a loving, talented, beautiful wife, who also loves and dreams water skiing and without whom this book would not be.

I dedicate this book to you, Chris, with love and thanks and wonderful memories. I only hope its readers will enjoy it as much as I did writing it with you.

ABOUT THE AUTHOR

Educated as a court reporter, Al Tyll was born in Troy, New York, the son of athletic-minded German-born parents, who brought him up with HEALTHY-BODY, SOUND-MIND philosophies. His dad, Alfred E. Tyll, won the New England Gymnastics Championship in 1932, the year the author was born.

Al Tyll first waterskied in 1954, and as he says in the book, "Don't be discouraged — I didn't even make it the first try." In 1959 he saw his first National Water Ski Tournament. In 1960 he qualified to enter, and placed 10th in Men's Tricks. In 1961, a torn cartilage prevented him from entering the nationals. In 1962, he won the Men's Tricks Event, and continued to win it in '63, '64, and '65, a formidable accomplishment for a Connecticut Court Reporter who only skis part time, five months out of the year! Yet, Al Tyll still finds time to design and endorse skis, trick handles, boats, and equipment; to run Al Tyll Enterprises at Bantam, Connecticut, a mail order house for superior custom water skiing equipment; to write magazine articles; to make radio, TV appearances; to serve on the Rules Committee of the American Water Ski Association; as Councilman from Connecticut and Rhode Island; as President of the progressive Connecticut Water Ski Association; and as Technical Advisor for the now-famous Bantam Lake Ski Club. (This editor just wants to know: When does he have time for practice?)

Described by the Water Skier as "magician" of trick skiing the author has probably done more for trick water skiing than any other person. In 1965, for instance, he didn't lose a tournament:

1. *Northeastern Men's Tricks Champion*
2. *Master's Men's Tricks Champion (record run: 4649.9 Points)*
3. *New England Men's Tricks Champion*
4. *National Men's Tricks Champion (to make it his fourth consecutive National Championship — something of a record)*

In the past five years no one can boast this record:
1962-63-64-65 National Men's Trick Skiing Champion
1961-62-63-64 North American Men's Trick Skiing Champion
1963 and 1965 Masters Men's Tricks Champion
1962-63-64-65 Eastern Regional Men's Tricks Champion
Seven Times Record Holder in Trick Skiing
First Trick Skier to crack the 4,000 point barrier.

Mr. Tyll has appeared in many national magazines having done features for POPULAR MECHANICS, BOYS LIFE, THE WATER SKIER, and MOTOR BOATING. He has also appeared in BOATING NEWS, WATERSKI & SMALLCRAFT MAGAZINE, SCINAUTICO, LOOK, WEST COAST BOATING NEWS, HOT BOAT, BOAT-O-RAMA, THE BOATING INDUSTRY, and many syndicated columns and newspapers throughout the world.

He has been seen many times on Sports Spectacular, Wide World of Sports, and Sports International, not to mention many TV appearances such as on TO TELL THE TRUTH, STORY OF AL TYLL and many regional appearances.

Chris and Al Tyll at work on book in trophy room.

ABOUT CHRIS TYLL

Originally from Pembroke, Mass., Chris began water skiing in 1959, first taking to jumping — later tricks. Noted throughout the East for her splendid style and form, she rarely leaves a tournament without one, two, or three trophies. In fact, since she still skis in all three events — slalom, jumping and tricks, the latest tally shows her to have two more trophies than her famous hubby; a sticky point with the champ who feels men should "always lead."

The attractive hazel-eyed blonde appeared in Life, Sat. Eve. Post and Look Magazines in the Hood Milk Physical Fitness Program; does part time modeling; helps run Al Tyll Enterprises; keeps in shape for tournament competition; and sometimes accompanies her husband on his appearances, "—always picking out the nice trips like Florida, or the West Indies."

Dubbed by her husband as "Chief Photographer" for the book project, Chris not only photographed the Champ's many sequence pictures — a relatively new experience for the 20 year old housewife — but skied for many sequences herself.

"And, oh yes," she adds, "All summer I'm 'Official Driver' which isn't easy. These champs are temperamental!"

TOURNAMENT RECORD — 1965
   Northeastern Championships, Scotia, New York:
      2nd — Women's Jumping
      3rd — Women's Slalom
      3rd — Women's Tricks
   Eastern Regional Championships, Reading, Pa.:
      3rd — Women's Jumping
   North Americans — Lake Placid, N.Y.:
      3rd — Women's Jumping
   Connecticut State Open, Highland Lake, Conn.
      1st — Women's Jumping
      2nd — Women's Tricks
   1964: North Eastern Championships, Scotia, N.Y.
      1st Place, Mixed Doubles.
      National Championships, Webster, Mass.,
      6th Place in Women's Jumping.
      Connecticut Open Championship,
      Highland Lake, Conn.
      1st Place Women's Jumping.
   1961: Rhode Island Open — 1st Place Girls Jumping.
      Mass. Open — 1st Place, Mixed Doubles.
   1960: Empire State Open, 1st Place, Mixed Doubles
   EXHIBITION: Jumping & Double Jumping,
      National Safe Boating Week,
      Middletown, Connecticut

CONTENTS

Fine and correct ingredients can make a difference. Trick skiing actually demands using best equipment.

First Things First

About the boat, the skis, the boat team, the rope, handle and binders.

UNTIL WINNING the 1962 National Men's Trick Skiing Championship, I never had a boat that would even come near tournament specifications. In fact, for the first six years of my water skiing experience I owned a small, light 14 footer with a wide transom powered by a 35-horse Johnson. But—I sure did a lot of water skiing! Therefore. . .

ABOUT THE BOAT

Anyone with a boat (12'-14' minimum) that can deep-water-start a skier (usually 25 hp or more) can actually become a proficient water skier—especially fun skiers and trick skiers. I emphasize tricks because slow tow speeds are necessary in this event (12-20 mph) making navigable bodies of water as small as 200 yards long by 75 yards wide usable for "tricking."

Towboats of 75 or more horsepower are necessary to maintain the higher speed and greater pull of slalom skiers and jumpers. Ideal towboats have a driver's seat facing forward, and one or more seats facing aft for observers. Lots of room astern is desirable for skis, ropes, handles, boarding ladders, etc. A ski tow hitch two to five feet ahead of the transom transmits the drag of the skier toward the center turning axis of the boat and minimizes lurching.

To avoid skiing in great prop turbulence, the beginner should use a standard 75-foot line. After graduating to wake tricks, he should shorten the rope so as to meet the wake at its sharpest, bubble-free point (usually 40 to 60 feet long).

I illustrate two boats that are perfect for water skiing connoisseurs: The Al Tyll Skier, by Correct Craft, and the Twin Johnson Powered Crosby Hull.

THE BOAT TEAM

Driver DRIVES! Observer OBSERVES!

A speed fluctuation of more than one mile per hour seriously impedes the performing skier—especially trick skiers. In the 1962 Masters at Callaway Gardens, Georgia, the boat driver pulled me at 17 mph rather than my required 18. My skis rode deeper in the water and I klobbered after a one-ski wake-stepover front-to-back, placing seventh for the day—that Masters being a no-fall tournament!

While breaking in a new driver, I check his accuracy at holding speed and rehearse with him and the observer the signals I use for better skier-to-boat communication. When "pulling out" a skier, accelerates moderately but steadily to the requested speed. Then hold that speed! Watch where you're going! Let the driver observe!

This is the Twin Johnson Powered Crosby Hull.

This is the Al Tyll Skier by Correct Craft. The author endorsed its many excellent skiing qualities.

Chris Tyll shows a pair of standard water skis.

STANDARD WATER SKIS

Skis most commonly used in pairs are about 66″ long, 6″-7″ wide, and ½″ to ¾″ thick. Each ski has a foot binder approximately in the middle of the ski, and a small keel under the tail. This keel provides stability and keeps the ski tracking well, much like the groove in a snow ski.

Most standard skis are manufactured and sold with rather inadequate adjustable binders (so that people of all foot sizes can use them) that are probably okay for the once-in-a-while water skier. Avid skiers and tournament competitors always customize their binders with thicker toe and heel pieces and wind up screwing them down to the ski in fixed (nonadjustable) position. This way the adjustment can never slip and the skier is always guaranteed the correct fit.

Water skis come in varying shapes and sizes between the (1) straight ski (straight parallel sides and square back) and (2) banana shape of varying widths, lengths and tapers.

Generally speaking, the straight ski can carry more weight at slower speeds with less motor power, but drags more at higher speeds.

The more streamlined banana shape offers less water resistance and handles better at higher speeds. (This is why most skiers use the tapered banana shape for their slalom ski.)

SELECT YOUR STANDARD SKIS AS FOLLOWS:

SKIER'S WEIGHT	SKI LENGTH	SKI WIDTH
40 to 80 lbs.	52″	5″-6″
70 to 200 lbs.	66″	6½″
170 to 300 lbs.	68″-72″	6½″-8″

THE ROPE

The standard and best length for skiing is 75 feet of strong, rigid line that floats, and has a breaking strength of more than 800 pounds. For all around water skiing, I recommend ¼″ diamond braid polyethylene or polypropylene.

Polyethylene will stretch the first few times used, but will soon take a "set" and become quite rigid. After that you'll feel little give when you pull on it.

Polypropylene, however (the official rope used in all AWSA sanctioned tournaments in jumping and slalom), has an elastic quality. A strong slalom skier can stretch a 75′ line two feet during his "cut." And, if he isn't prepared, when it recoils it could throw him for a loop forward. It

Close-up of standard line; has 800 lb. strength.

took me a long time to get accustomed to it. Tournament experts feel that as skiers get used to this stretch-recoil situation, they may use it to their advantage; i.e. more points in the slalom course; and longer jumps.

There's no doubt that jumpers get more footage with polypropylene. Observers feel that polypropylene line was responsible for the three young women, Barbara Klack, Dixie Hoyt, and Liz Allen, reaching the 100-foot mark in the Women's and Girl's jumping events. Before polypropylene was used, the gals just couldn't leap that far. There's no doubt but that it snaps you right off the ramp.

In tricks, however, where quick tugs, wraps and various difficult rope handling is entailed, I prefer a nonrecoil line. In fact I use $\frac{5}{16}''$ braided polyethylene. Many competitors I know use $\frac{3}{8}''$. One of my friends and close training companions, Howie Mitchell, chortles: "Man, if steel cable would float, I'd use *it* for tricks! I like that solid feel."

THE HANDLE

Although many skiers still use the double handles, it is completely out in competition as far as I have seen, and the single handle is being widely used and adopted. Handle lengths vary from 11″ to 18″; diameters from 1 to 1¼″. They are usually constructed of wood, aluminum, plastic, or rubber, and combinations thereof.

There is no handle made that surpasses the superiority, comfort, and durability of the Glad Hand-le, a soft rubber-coated aluminum core with soft plastic ends, that is rapidly becoming a status symbol of the sport. I think so highly of it that I use it on all my custom AL TYLL Trik Toehold Handles.

GRIPPING THE HANDLE

There are two basic ways to hold the handle; the standard "knuckles on top" fashion and the "baseball-bat" fashion.

The first method is a comfortable, relaxed position for easy skiing.

The "baseball-bat" grip should be used during strenuous pulls, as in slalom and jumping. During hard pulls, the skier often brings the handle in close toward his left or right hip, depending on the direction he is "cutting." (If he is making a left turn, his left hip; a right turn, his right hip.) The "baseball-bat" grip is a more vise-like grip for these purposes.

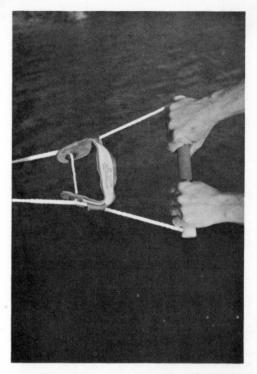

Knuckles-on-top on Al Tyll Trik Toehold Handle.

Baseball bat grip on the standard Glad Hand-le.

BINDERS

Your water ski binders can make or break your skiing, for these are what connect you with the skis—what transmits your pressures, or gentle nudges. I've often said, "I want the ski to be a part of my foot." If there's the slightest play, looseness, pinch, or pain, it can hamper your best performances. And on this question I must be frank. Most manufacturers put junk on their skis! There is also a sickening variety of adjustment devices which vary the distance of the heel unit from the toepiece. Most of these are sloppy, heavy, breakable sandtraps designed by some third rate machinist's helper who didn't even know how to water ski. I'm sorry, but I'm bitter about this subject. But because of this I'm afraid we've lost many many potential water skiers. Have you ever tried skiing on two freeboards? (Plain skis without binders). You might just as well, for that's about how well most commercial binders hold your feet.

You can bet your binders that you won't see one champion skier using commercial adjustable binders. And, you can also assume that that guy or gal has spent many hours getting his or her binder to fit and hold just right. I know that my wife, Chris, and I constantly work on our binders. (Chris won't even ski on a new ski without first mounting her custom binders on them.) And she's right. She'd never appreciate the fine characteristics of the ski without good foot-to-ski connection.

So I shall make a prediction: In years to come water skis will be sold blank, without binders. There will be several sizes and types of binders to choose from. As with snow skis, the sports store operator or shop mechanic will mount the binders for you.

I illustrate three fine binders available for custom purchase on the market today.

No. 1. The Tourney-Kit. Used by many champs, with variations, this binder set is fixed (nonadjustable). Usually the ski comes with just the toepiece mounts. You mount the heel unit by screwing the metal heel "U," which holds the high heel rubber, right down to the ski. A soft, comfortable ¼" thick composition rubber is used. If adjustment is required, the old holes must be filled and new holes drilled.

No. 2. The Tourney-Pro Binder. This is a fixed binder using a 6½" high heelpiece of thick "Formulastic" composition (almost ⅜"). It is soft, but sturdy and the toepieces come in two sizes. The heel unit can be adjusted by removing the center screw of each rail. The manufacturer (Superior Sports Specialties) uses attractive, lightweight gold anodized aluminum hardware, so as not to add much dead weight to the ski.

No. 3. The Holdex Binder. Invented by my good friend, Tony Kluge, of Rego Park, New York, this is the binder of the future, and is now being marketed by him in limited production. It has many superior ramifications. The greatest feature is a double layer of rubber across the instep, which is connected to the ski by a nonresilient, adjustable strap. By tightening this strap the heel is prevented from pulling out of the heelpiece, an unwanted occurrence that has plagued water skiers for years. In addition, Mr. Kluge places a second rubber re-enforcement over the nub of the heel (against the Achillies tendon) for the same reason. Of course, the binder still releases with a bad spill, but it sure doesn't come off unless you want it to, and gives you perfect control of the ski.

The Tourney-Pro; Tourney-Kit and Holdex binders.

Single ski Holdex binders mounted for display.

A LESSON IN BOAT DRIVING

(While towing a skier)

1. **Always drive the boat** in a straight line while the skier is performing (tricks, slalom, or jumping).

2. When you have to turn, signal the skier with a circular motion of your hand held high, so he prepares for the turn.

3. Then make a neat 50- to 80-yard turn circle.

4. End it approximately where you started it. This will bring you back in the center of your previous wake; you'll miss all of the rough water caused by your own boat on the first pass.

5. After one complete cycle, your path will have formed a "Barbell" outline. It's easy and safe and always gives the skier smooth water. The straight "Bar" part of the course should be at least 350 yards long for optimum skier performance. Of course, you must be guided and governed by the size of your water practice area.

NOTE: This is the reason why there is never rough water in a regulation slalom course, or jump course, because the official drivers always follow this pattern. •

Always drive in straight line when skier performs.

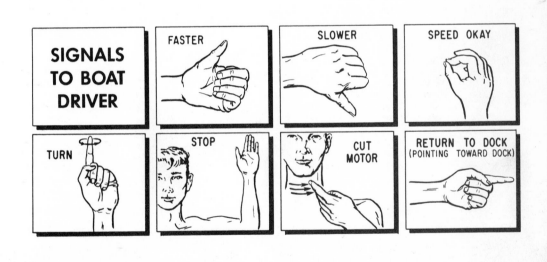

BARBELL DRIVING COURSE

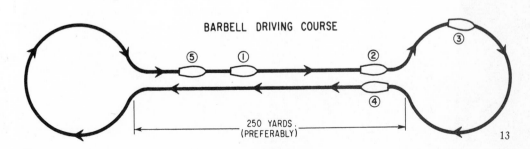

250 YARDS.
(PREFERABLY)

Fun Skiing

Getting up on two skis, crossing and jumping the wakes, using one ski.

Binders are important. Make sure they fit well.

Get the feel of standing on skis, the rope's pull.

Learn to stand, arms up, knees flexed for action.

Get in waist-deep water. Wearing ski belt, with binders snug, take position shown and you're ready.

GETTING UP ON TWO SKIS

Get in waist-deep water. Wear a ski belt. Put your skis on. Binders snug.
1. Assume crouch position.
   a. Knees bent.
   b. Ski tips peeking out of water, one foot apart.
   c. Arms straight.
   d. Tell driver to put boat in slow forward idle.
2. Yell "Hit it."
   a. Driver should begin steady acceleration to 20 mph.
   b. Freeze in starting crouch position.
   c. Lean slightly against pull of boat.
   d. Try to stay over binders.
3. Stay in crouch position as skis begin to surface.
   a. You may straighten your knees a bit—but just a bit.
   b. Arms still straight.
   c. Body over binders.
4. At 20 mph skis ride high and easy.
   a. Stay in vertical crouch position for a while until you gain confidence.
   b. Keep arms straight.
5. After a minute or so straighten knees almost fully.
   a. Arms straight.
   b. Skis a foot apart.
   c. Straighten your back. Try to relax. Ride directly behind the boat for a while.
   d. If it is your first time, don't ski longer than five minutes; especially older persons.

AL TYLL ATTEMPT RATIO: 1 to 6 tries

Lean slightly against accelerating speed of boat.

Stay in crouch position as skis begin to surface.

At 20 mph the skis ride high and easy. Stay in vertical crouch position until you gain confidence.

After a minute or so, straighten knees almost fully. Relax. Ski directly behind boat—don't overdo it.

The author demonstrates the Skee Trainer to two young ladies. Device is simple, very easy to use.

AN EVEN EASIER WAY—
THE SKEE TRAINER

An ingenious device! The Skee Trainer actually holds your skis rigid—your body in correct low crouch position. Designed by my good friend, Stew Leonard, it is available through Skee Trainer, Inc., Norwalk, Connecticut ($9.95 for adults; $6.95 for small fry), and comes in real handy at a Sunday afternoon "ski" party—when you've got to take lots of friends and relatives skiing. I've seen Stew teach some pretty uncoordinated people and very young children with his device, which attaches easily to any rope and handle.

1. Get in waist-deep water.
   a. Slip the Skee Trainer over your ski tips.
   b. Spread your skis as far apart as possible.
   c. Knees bent.
   d. Arms bent around your knees.
   e. Press down firmly on the handle.
   f. As driver accelerates to 20 mph—freeze.
2. Allow Skee Trainer to slip off ski tips, by:
   a. Relieving down pressure on handle.
   b. Stay low.
   c. Let arms straighten slowly.
   d. Keep body weight over binders.
3. Relax and straighten up slowly.
   a. Arms straight.
   b. Skis a foot apart.
   c. Stay inside the wakes.

NOTE: Don't ski longer than five minutes—if it's your first time out. Especially the "desk set."

AL TYLL ATTEMPT RATIO: First try! Well, you should!

Child squats lower, but end result is the same.

Press down to hold skis, lift up to release them.

Straighten up slowly, use Trainer as tow handle.

In waist-deep water, slip Skee Trainer over skis.

19

CROSSING THE WAKE

Many beginners, after first getting up on skis, try to cross the wake improperly by drifting slowly toward it, getting one ski over the wake, and then trying to get the other ski over. They inevitably get "hung up" on the wake, as in the "wrong way" picture.

1. Skiing in the center of the wakes,
   a. Hold handle "baseball-bat" fashion.
   b. Pull in arms slightly.
   c. Lean in the direction of the wake you wish to cross.
   d. You should meet the wake under power so that you'll easily carry over and beyond it.

2. On the wake,
   a. Skier's knees bend more as the "bump" of the wake is felt.
   b. Stay low. Don't stand tall.
   c. Skis a foot apart and parallel.
   d. Keep weight directly over binders.

3. Having crossed the wake,
   a. Relax out there for a while.
   b. If you wish to return, stay low and proceed back the same way.

NOTE: Practicing this simple technique, you can begin a "slalom rhythm" back and forth across both wakes. (Jumpers use this technique to gain speed approaching ramp.)

TYLL ATTEMPT RATIO: Nothing to it!

WRONG: skier drifted to wake, got "hung up" on it.

Pull in, lean toward wake, cut across as shown.

RIGHT: use baseball grip, ski in center of wake.

Stay outside a while, relax, then cut back across.

Up on two skis, binders snug, about 20 mph speed.

Select firmest foot for skiing, lift the other one.

SKIER'S SALUTE

Get up on two skis with binders snug. Tell boat driver "20 mph." Ride with skis about one foot apart.

1. Slowly shift weight to one ski.
2. Slowly pick up the "salute" ski about six inches off the water. Make sure you keep its front tip from catching or digging in the water. Ride this way for several seconds until you feel steady.
3. Raise front tip of "salute" ski higher (to a 45-degree angle or better) by bringing knee in tightly toward chest. Letting go of the handle on the "salute" side seems to make the trick easier—and looks better, too.

NOTE: Try lifting first one ski and then the other, to determine which foot is steadier on the ski. From then on, this will be your "slalom" or one-ski foot.

AL TYLL ATTEMPT RATIO: 1 to 5 tries

Letting go of handle on salute side makes trick easier—and looks much better.

21

JUMPING THE WAKES

Wake jumping is exciting fun. Depending upon the size of the boat wakes, skiers can get as high as three or four feet in the air; and, with enough of a "cut" can easily clear both wakes. The best wake jumps are from the outside of the wakes inward, as most wakes have a steeper take-off angle on the outside. The longer your approach to the wake, the higher and farther you'll jump. With a little practice you'll easily clear both wakes.

1. Start cutting hard toward the wake.
   a. Use "baseball-bat" grip.
   b. Pull in on handle (and keep it in during cut).
   c. Crouch very low and cut.

(Jumpers use this style in their double wake cut toward the jump.)

2. As you hit the wake, pop upward, snapping your knees straight.
3. In the air,
   a. Keep tips up.
   b. Try to keep body weight over binders.

(Some skiers like to assume "soldier" straight style, as Chris is demonstrating. Others like to bend forward at the waist. Adopt your own style. It should be pleasing and controlled.)

4. Landing.
   a. Bend at knees and waist for a low, steady, solid landing.
   b. Land with skis well apart, parallel.

TYLL ATTEMPT RATIO: "Very easy"

Start from outside wakes, cut hard toward them.

"Pop" as you hit wake, snapping knees straight.

Chris Tyll assumes "soldier style" as she pops into air after leaving wake crest. Keep ski tips up.

Bend at knees and waist for low, solid landing. Land with skis well apart and parallel as shown here.

KICKING OFF ONE SKI

Suggested speed: 22 mph. Start off on two skis. Leave the "kick-off" ski's binder very loose. Ride along on two skis about a foot apart.

1. Slowly shift your weight to your "slalom" foot.
   a. "Kick-off" ski's binder should be very loose.
   b. Raise heel almost out of "kick-off" ski.
2. Bend knee lifting foot off ski.
   a. "Kick-off" ski will trail off to your rear.
   b. Hold still for a few seconds.
3. Drag free foot in water for extra balance.
4. After a few moments, place free foot behind "ski foot."
   a. Lean back and relax.
   b. Ski that way for a few minutes before you try anything else.

AL TYLL ATTEMPT RATIO: 1 to 5 tries

On two skis, slowly shift weight to "slalom" foot.

Kick-off ski binder should be **very** loose. After balancing on one foot—bend knee lifting other out.

Drag free foot in water for extra balance here.   After a few moments, place free foot behind other.

Riding one ski and cutting back and forth is called "slaloming." See pages 28-33 for this technique.

GETTING UP ON ONE SKI

Get in waist-deep water. Wear a ski belt. Put one ski on your slalom foot—binder very snug.

1. Bring "ski knee" in close to your chest. Drag free foot directly behind you, toes pointed—like a rudder.
2. Tell driver, "In gear." Get the feel of being pulled slowly (2 to 4 mph) in this starting position. When everything feels right and you are in proper balance in the water, yell "Hit it" and freeze. Keep only a slight bend in your arms.
3. Freeze in that starting position. As the ski starts to surface, you may straighten your knee just a bit, but not too much. Don't try to stand up too soon. Drag your free foot behind you for balance.
4. When the ski is riding nicely, bring the trailing foot forward and place it directly behind the front foot, on the ski.
5. Lean back and relax. •

AL TYLL ATTEMPT RATIO: 1 to 5 tries

Get in waist-deep water, bring ski knee in close to chest, drag free foot behind, toes pointed back.

Tell driver, "In gear!" Get the feel of being pulled slowly, 2 to 4 mph; when balanced, yell, "Hit it!"

Freeze in starting position as boat speeds up and you start to surface. Drag foot behind for balance.

When riding nicely, bring the rear foot forward.

Place free foot behind ski foot; relax and enjoy!

Slaloming

Water Skier Magazine

A right angle cut can send up a wall of water some 20 to 30 feet high as shown in the photo, above.

Using one ski to send up a wall of water in those sharp cuts and turns.

SLALOM SKIS

Used both for the great fun of sharp turns or "cuts," and in competitions negotiating the regulation slalom course, slalom skis come in varying shapes and sizes, 60" to 70" long and 6½" to 8" wide! A slalom ski usually has a front and rear binder as both feet are placed on the ski, and a deep (3" to 6") stabilizing tail fin or keel. All the designs I have mentioned for regular water skis have been tried on slalom skis, but the most popular is the bullet-shaped tip with an extreme taper toward the tail. This taper usually begins in the vicinity of the front binder, narrowing all the way to the tail. With this design of ski, the skier can turn or "cut" the ski at almost right angles, sending up an impressive wall of water 20

to 30 feet high during the turn, after which he accelerates to exhilarating speed across the wakes, where he banks for a similar cut in the reverse direction.

In recent years the concave slalom ski has fascinated the tournament world. A concave curve is milled into the bottom of the ski from tip to tail, usually amounting to ⅛" to ¼" at the center. The theories go that this acts much like the grooves in snow skis, making for steadier tracking and steeper cuts. Many of the champs I've spoken to are noncommittal. Some say they could do just as well on straight blanks— but nevertheless they use the concave in competition.

Most competition slaloms have a quarter-round bevel all the way around the bottom edges of the ski. This makes the ski ride lower in the water, causing it to drag a bit more, but results in a much steadier, more controllable, sharper-cutting ski. By the same token, as the skis get smaller, and as bevels get more pronounced, the harder it is to pull slalom skiers out of the water with low-horsepower boats. But, who cares? The guy who loves man-sized slalom likes speed, and needs a high-powered boat anyway. In slalom skiing especially, the need for the fast, powerful boat is accentuated, because any 185-pounder on a tapered ski, cutting with all his might behind a 40- or 50-horsepower boat, can slow the boat down 4 to 6 miles per hour.

Correct binder placement on the slalom ski is important to get optimum performance. If your weight is too far forward on the ski, its tip may dive, or the tail might pop out of the water on a cut. If your weight is too far aft, causing the tip to ride too far out of the water, you'll lose the benefit of the full ski's edge which helps the ski keep tracking well, and helps hold it in the water on turns.

There are so many good slalom skis on the market, more than jumpers or trick skis, many companies selling various sizes and designs, that you'll just have to try several of them out and decide for yourself. Make sure they have good, thick, binders with high heel-pieces. And, remember, always wear a life vest or a ski when slaloming.

Slalom ski has double binders for one-ski action.

ONE SKI TURNS OR "CUTS"

After you've ridden one ski for several minutes, try turning first one way, then the other—but stay inside the wakes at first. Suggested speed: 24 to 26 mph.

SIMPLE TURNS

In good, comfortable position, weight equally on each foot, lean in the direction you wish to travel.

To bank or turn to the left, lean in that direction. The left edge of the ski will cut into the water deeper, guiding the ski in that direction. To stop your turn, stop leaning.

THE HARD CUT

The harder you lean, the faster you'll turn in that direction. It is simply a matter of how much on edge that ski is. But there's more to hard cutting than the lean. Rhythm, pull, timing, acceleration and deceleration must all be coordinated. Let's go through a hard cut, using a buoy as a reference point.

Here Chris Tyll executes a simple slalom turn.

A hard cut throws up more water, is leaned into.

CUTTING AROUND A SLALOM BUOY

Timing, turning, acceleration, braking, and "aiming" the next turn are important factors here, and must always be done in that order.

1. Approach buoy wide, no slack in rope.
   a. Weight toward front foot.
   b. Bend forward at the waist.
   c. Inside hand, holding handle, extended, for better reach.
   d. Free hand outward for balance.
2. Turn begins, even before passing buoy.
   a. Bring upper torso back.
   b. Pull handle in toward waist.
   c. Keep pressure on the rope.
   d. Cut very close to down-course side of buoy.
3. The "Cut"
   a. Grasp handle quickly with both hands for stronger cut.
   b. Pull and cut hard to the first wake.

PREPARING FOR THE NEXT BUOY OR TURN

   a. **Stop cutting** at center of wakes.
   b. Bring weight forward again.
   c. Let go with outside arm.
   d. While decelerating, extend handle (inside) arm for long reach.
   e. Approach buoy wide.

RUNNING THE SLALOM COURSE

(Standard rope length: 75 ft.)

1. **Before entering** the course, swing out to the left side of the wake, eyes on gate buoys.
2. As boat enters course, drift through the gate at an angle.
3. That will position you 8 to 10 ft. outside the first slalom buoy.
4. Cut back toward the left just missing that buoy on its down-course side.
5. Pull hard to the center of the wake.
6. Ease up and decelerate, preparing for opposite turn around Buoy No. 2.
7. Aim your path wider (to the left) than the second buoy.
8. You again cut the second buoy close. Repeat this for the next four buoys. Pass through the end boat gate.

REMEMBER: Practice makes perfect.

Approach buoy wide, no slack in rope, lean in.

Inside hand holds handle, other out for balance.

Begin turn before passing buoy, pull on handle.

Grasp quickly with both hands for stronger cut.

In competition, slalom skier leans hard to the left as he rounds a right buoy, will now cross wake.

Water Skier photos

Rhythm, pull, timing, acceleration and deceleration must all be coordinated by both skier and boat team.

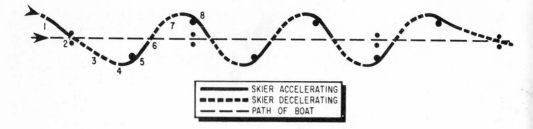

```
━━━━━━ SKIER ACCELERATING
■■■■■■ SKIER DECELERATING
─ ─ ─ ─ PATH OF BOAT
```

"SHORT LINE" SLALOM

If you enter competition and successfully make 36 mph (or 34 mph if you're not in the Men's Division) these hints might help you when you shorten your line:

12 FT. OFF: No problem. Seems hardly different from 75 ft.

18 FT. OFF: Your normal cutting strength will tend to accelerate you faster across the wake, and you'll have deceleration problems. Don't cut quite so long.

24 AND 30 FT. OFF: You must ski more precisely, make your turns sharper, and shorten your "cut" time even more. The shorter rope increases your "cut" angle.

HOW TO PRACTICE RHYTHMIC SLALOM *WITHOUT A COURSE*

Very few of us are lucky enough to have our own slalom course. And, of course, don't ever think of winning slalom competitions without having practiced considerably on a course.

You can, however, improve yourself a great deal by rhythmic slalom "cut" practice even though it is not on an official slalom course. At least you'll become very proficient at handling your ski, which is the first "must" in slalom. You can also work on your timing.

1. Practice behind a powerful, fast boat at increasing speeds. But, start off at a comfortable 26 or 28 mph.
2. Tell your driver to always drive straight and steady.

3. Ski out about 40 feet from the center of the wake.
4. Make a strong "cut."
5. Stop your "cut" at the center of the wake.
6. Lean forward and decelerate to a point about 40 feet on the other side—then cut back again, and so on.

REMEMBER:

a. When cutting, pull handle in toward waist and lean your upper torso against pull.

b. Upon deceleration or "braking," bend forward at waist and switch weight forward.

SLALOM COMPETITION

Slalom starting speeds for the various divisions are as follows:

Speed	Division
30	Boys and Men
28	Senior Men
26	Junior Boys
26	Girls
26	Women
26	Senior Women
24	Junior Girls

The judges can lower the starting speeds 2-4 mph, or raise them 2 mph. With each subsequent pass, the boat speed is raised 2 mph. After 34 mph is reached (or 36 mph in the Mens and Boys Divisions) the rope is shortened, first 12 feet, then in 6-foot increments until all skiers are eliminated. The one who negotiates the most consecutive buoys wins. In case of a tie the skier who scores the most total buoys, wins. If there is still a tie, a runoff is held.

An official slalom course layout is shown. Instructions on laying one out can be obtained from American Water Ski Assn. •

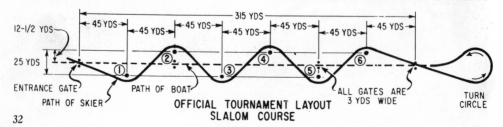

OFFICIAL TOURNAMENT LAYOUT
SLALOM COURSE

Evinrude photo

Learners should wear life belt, make simple turns.

Florida State photo

To bank or turn to left, lean in that direction.

Wet suits are popular for practice sessions in bad weather or during the off-season to offset the chill.

FPG photo

Champion Al Tyll and Women's World Champion Liz Allan at Orlando, Fla.

Trick Skiing

Step-by-step photos and instructions of all the tricks in the book!

TRICK SKIS

I use arc-type skis, 8″ wide with blunt ends. They have no stabilizing fins—just a smooth bottom—and can ski backward and sideways, as well as forward. They're great fun and enable the skier to do gymnastic tricks on the water.

For instance, the new Trik Star, which I designed for Taperflex (Superior Sports Specialties) is of exact symmetrical design, curving up equally on either end. The ski bottom has a slight dihedral to prevent edge catching when the ski is sidesliding or turning. It took me three years to arrive at the best curve for my arc of a perfect circle design. To my amazement, even the top edges of a trick ski have to be taken into consideration, so I bevel them like an airplane wing to make the ski streamlined

—no matter which direction it is turning. The Taperflex engineers suggested, "why don't you balance it?" So we thinned down the tips and beefed up the center and thanks to them we now have 70% of the total weight of the trick ski under foot—a terrific advantage on stepovers and precision wake turns. The ski became lighter, yet more rigid and the total ski's weight was easier to control. You see, a camber-like bend or flex forces the trick skier to constantly change his stance, or rotating axis, making tricks rough and shaky.

Trick skiers should select their ski sizes as follows:

SKIER'S WEIGHT	TRICK SKI LENGTH	TRICK SKI WIDTH
Under 100 lbs.	36″	7″
100-150 lbs.	48″	8″
150 and up	52″	8″

Chris shows Trik Star skis designed by Al Tyll.

THE TRIK (TOEHOLD) HANDLE

(Also known as TOE STRAP, TOE TRAP, FOOTHOLD, etc.)

For years trick skiers used a primitive strap tied between the two ropes holding the handle. This rough, crude method just would not hold. With the slightest jerk or slack in the line, off came the handle. Then Stew Leonard, a fine trick skier, from Norwalk, Connecticut, invented a "U" shaped toehold held just in front of the handle by a short crosspiece between the handle lines. This simulates a sling that actually snugs up on the skier's toes. Should the skier fall, he merely points his toes and off comes the handle. I developed an improved version for my own use in competition using comfortable suede-like latigo leather, and began winning competitions like crazy. Hundreds of skiers wanted my "Trik Handle" so I acquired the patent rights and began making a custom-fit version—The Al Tyll Trik Handle ($14.25). Later I licensed Superior Sports Specialties of San Fernando, California, to manufacture an inexpensive version using 2″ webbing—The Al Tyll Toe Trap ($6.95). These toehold trick handles are the secret of good toehold tricks, especially difficult ones like the wake-toehold-three-sixty.

ABOUT THE PHOTOS

In these sequence pictures, I demonstrate most of the basic tricks in one direction, off the left wake. Being left-footed, I do my front-backs to the left (counterclockwise)—my back-fronts to the right (clockwise). I've learned all three-sixties and "helicopters" in both directions, off either wake, and highly recommend you practice the reverse of the trick as soon as you've mastered it in one direction.

Should you be a right-footed skier, you'll prefer the right wake and will do your front-backs to the right; your back-front to the left. In other words, vice versa. However, the same instructions apply.

THE AL TYLL ATTEMPT RATIO

At the beginning of the instructions for each trick you'll find the official AWSA point value (as of Jan. 1, 1966) for the maneuver. Ranging from 20 to over 350 points per trick, these values are a good indication of the difficulty of each particular one.

Some skiers learn faster than others, however. So, I'll also give my own "rating" as to the range of attempts or tries it takes average skiers to make the trick properly. Now, don't hold me to it.* It took me over 500 falls (2½ years) before I could make the Wake Toe 360 with reasonable consistency. I figured that was the world's hardest trick until California's Dennis Ralves tried it, and made it on the 12th try!

If you don't make the trick somewhere within my "Attempt Ratio" study the instructions and pictures again. You must be doing something wrong. GOOD LUCK.

*My "attempt ratio" assumes that you're learning the tricks in the chronological order in which they are placed in this book and would be inaccurate should you attempt a difficult trick before you learn the simpler ones.

This is the Al Tyll Trik Handle—by the author.

Assume vertical crouch position; arms, knees bent.

For sideslide to left, bounce up, release hand.

TWO-SKI SIDESLIDE
20 POINTS

Use a 75-ft. line. Get the best pair of trick skis obtainable. Select a speed between 15 mph and 20 mph that feels best to you.

1. Assume vertical crouch position. Knees bent. Head up. Arms slightly bent. When tricking never let your ams out straight all the way. Start bouncing slightly up and down by bending the knees.

2. For a sideslide to the left, bounce upward—simultaneously releasing your left hand, turning leftward.

3. Your skis will slip into the sideslide position. This will feel slippery, so keep your two skis about 10 to 12 inches apart for more stability. Keep their leading edges up; trailing edges down. Angle your knees away from the boat's pull to keep from catching an edge. Keep your free hand to the rear for balance.

AL TYLL ATTEMPT RATIO: 1 to 10 tries

Keep skis 10 to 12 in. apart, leading edges up; angle knees away from boat's pull; balance with arm.

TWO-SKI 180 OR FRONT-TO-BACK

30 POINTS

1. **Ski directly behind** the boat in vertical crouch position.
   a. Knees bent.
   b. Head up.
   c. Arms slightly bent.
2. Bounce upward slightly.
   a. Release left hand.
   b. Leading head toward the left.
   c. Skis about 10 inches apart.
3. Right hand pulls handle toward right hip.
4. Approaching 180 position:
   a. Grasp handle with both hands.
   b. Keep head up, looking at horizon.
   c. Keep handle in close, almost touching the small of your back.
   d. Stay low, over binders.
   NOTE: After your first successful "180," ride backward for a while in Step 4 position to "get the feel." And—relax!

AL TYLL ATTEMPT RATIO: 3 to 10 tries

Assume vertical crouch position; arms, knees bent.

Bounce upward slightly, releasing your left hand.

Pull right hand toward right hip as you turn.

Finally, grasp handle with both hands, head up.

TWO-SKI BACK-TO-FRONT

30 POINTS

1. **Ski backward** in vertical crouch position.
   a. Head up.
   b. Handle in close.
   c. Knees bent.
   d. Skis one foot apart.
   e. Start "bouncing" in the knees.
2. At the "up" part of a slight bounce:
   a. Right hand lets go.
   b. Left hand holds handle in close.
   c. Stay directly over your binders.
3. For the last 90 degrees:
   a. Keep handle in close.
   b. Stay low.

4. Turn is completed.
   a. Keep head erect.
   b. Grasp handle with both hands as soon as possible.

AL TYLL ATTEMPT RATIO: 3 to 8 tries

THREE-SIXTY or "Tournaround"

40 POINTS

TO DO A THREE-SIXTY—FOLLOW ALL THE DIRECTIONS FOR THE "FRONT TO BACK" AND "BACK TO FRONT". JUST DON'T STOP IN THE "180" POSITION. KEEP YOUR HANDLE IN CLOSE. KNEES BENT. HEAD ERECT.

AL TYLL ATTEMPT RATIO: 5 to 15 tries

Ski backward in vertical crouch position, above.

At the up part of a slight bounce, let hand go.

For the last 90° keep handle in close, stay low.

When turn is completed, grasp handle for finish.

Spill-saving gimmick is to practice with weight.

A 35 lb. weight on a rope and pulley works well.

PRACTICING ROPE HANDLING

Practice, the champ says, makes perfect skiing.

Every time "Robert Ropetangle" gets into the front-to-back position, he falls backward toward the boat. Before dunking, his arms are straight behind him, straining like he's trying to pull the boat backward. He bowls over on his nose like a tenpin. If his handle had been held close, knuckles touching the small of his back, he'd still be there skiing backward.

An ideal spill-saving training gimmick is to rig a ski rope and pulley with a 35-pound weight on it, in your cellar, playroom, or outside on the lawn. This simulates the pull of the boat, teaching you rope handling without nuisance falls. Spin quickly, passing the rope in close, hand to hand, and you'll become nimble and sure. And, watch your muscles develop!

(Editor's Note: In late November of 1962, the author was invited to compete in the Western Hemisphere International Championships to be held in early December, at Miami. There was ice on Bantam Lake. Tyll had not trained in two months. Using this simple rope and pulley rig, the "Champ" trained for ten days on his frozen lawn, flew to Florida for the weekend, and won the Men's Tricks Championship!)

Assume vertical crouch, drift toward the wake.

At crest of wake hop briskly, left hand lets go.

As you bounce into the air, pull handle over hip.

WAKE TRICKS

You are now ready for wake tricks. Shorten your rope length 15 to 25 feet so that you'll meet the wake at its sharpest, most bubble-free, point. Most trick skiers like rope lengths between 45 to 60 feet. For a wake trick to be legal in competition, your skis must visibly leave the wake and be in the air during the turn. For instance, you can't slide the last quarter turn; or do the trick without getting into the air. Understand?

If your front-to-backs are counterclockwise (to the left), start from the center and use the left wake. For clockwise front-to-backs, use the right wake.

TWO-SKI WAKE FRONT-TO-BACK OR "WAKE 180"

50 POINTS

1. **Assume vertical crouch.** Drift toward the wake.
2. As you reach the crest of the wake:
   a. Hop briskly, but not higher than 8″.
   b. Left hand lets go. Right hand keeps handle in close.
3. As you bounce into the air:
   a. Right hand pulls handle over hip.
   b. Keep head up and turn quickly.
   c. Left hand reaches for handle.
4. Landing.
   a. Grasp handle again with both hands.
   b. "Give" in the knees upon landing to assume a low crouch position again.
   THE "TRICK" TO THIS TRICK: Stay low, but over your binders; knees bent. Don't jump too high. Turn quickly in the air. Ski neat!!

AL TYLL ATTEMPT RATIO: 5 to 20 tries

Landing: grasp handle with both hands; ski neat!

Assume backward crouch 6 ft. outside left wake.

Bounce briskly at crest, leading turn with head.

Turning in air: pull skis up a bit to clear wake.

Landing, front position; knees begin to "give."

TWO-SKI WAKE BACK-TO-FRONT, OR "WAKE FRONT"

50 POINTS

1. **Assume** backward vertical crouch position about six feet outside left wake.
   a. Drift in toward wake.
   b. Keep handle in close.
2. As you reach the crest:
   a. Bounce briskly, leading turn to the right with your head.
   b. Left hand lets go of handle.

3. Turning in the air:
   a. Head is facing forward—has already led turn fully.
   b. Pull skis up a bit to make sure they clear the wake.
4. Landing in front position:
   a. Skier's left hand is ready to grasp the handle.
   b. Knees begin to "give" with landing.
   NOTE: Don't cut back too hard toward wake. DRIFT! Stay low. Keep your skis 8" to 12" apart.

AL TYLL ATTEMPT RATIO: 3 to 10 tries

BACK-START ON TWO SKIS

16 POINTS (Neophyte trick)

1. **Get in waist-deep** water. Assume proper starting position, knees in toward chest. Tell driver "In gear," and "slow."
2. As boat idles forward at 2 or 3 mph, do a "180" in the water.
3. Grasp handle and hold it directly behind your thighs. Dunk your head in the water. After your head goes in the water, the driver should wait 2 or 3 seconds, then begin accelerating steadily to a speed of 18 mph. These few seconds should give you time to "get set."
4. As boat accelerates keep body rigid; knees slightly bent. The backs of your skis will come out of the water. Don't lean too far against the boat's pull; otherwise you'll go on your face. Stay low.
5. When surfaced, pull handle up against the small of your back, and assume a good, low vertical crouch, head up.

AL TYLL ATTEMPT RATIO: 3 to 8 tries

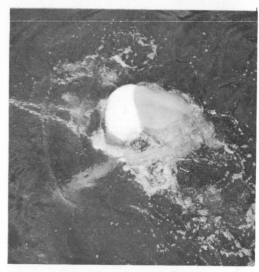

Grasp handle behind thighs, dunk head, get set.

TO START, assume position, above. See below.

As boat moves slowly, do a "180" turn in water.

As boat accelerates, keep body rigid, knees bent.

When surfaced, crouch, pull handle against back.

42

BEFORE DOING ONE-SKI TRICKS

1. **Make sure** you have a good pair of trick skis—48″ long for 150 pounders or under; and 52″ long for skiers weighing over 150.
2. YOUR BINDERS SHOULD BE COMFORTABLE AND VERY SNUG. THERE SHOULD BE NO PLAY BETWEEN FOOT AND SKI. IT SHOULD NOT COME OFF TOO EASILY. IF YOUR HEEL PULLS OUT EASILY, GET A ¼″ HIGH HEEL RUBBER. DON'T ADJUST THE BINDERS WHEN THEY ARE DRY. IF YOU DO THEY'LL BE VERY LOOSE WHEN WET.

MOUNTING THE BACK BINDER ON YOUR ONE-TRICK SKI FOR ONE-SKI TRICKS

a. Put the ski on the floor.
b. Place front foot in the binder.
c. Place your rear foot on the ski *close behind* the front foot.
d. Without watching your feet, turn your rear foot to the angle at which it feels most comfortable.
e. Draw a crayon or chalk mark, around your rear foot, on the ski.
f. Place your back binder accordingly.
NOTE: Left-foot-forward skiers find their rear foot most comfortable when it is pointing diagonally toward the right 15 to 40 degrees. (And vice versa for right-foot-forward skiers).

Make sure to put your rear foot close to the front foot. Keeping your total weight concentrated near the center of the trick ski assures optimum ski performance.

The author in a classic one-ski backward swan.

Comfortable, snug binders are a must for tricks.

Whether right-foot-forward or left-foot-forward, place second foot where comfortable and make mark.

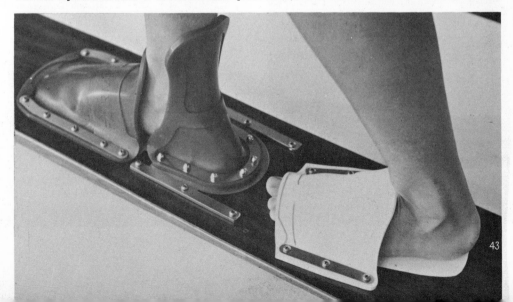

43

For one-ski sideslide, assume a vertical crouch.

ONE-SKI SIDESLIDE
70 POINTS

Learn to ride your one trick ski as a slalom ski before you try any tricks. Even practice mild cuts and wake jumping at a comfortable speed (usually 15 to 21 mph).

Try this trick in very smooth water, directly behind the boat, using a 75-ft. line.
1. Assume vertical crouch position.
2. Looking at the water just in front of your ski, bounce slightly, releasing your left hand and turning leftward.
3. When ski reaches sideslide position, it will be a slippery sensation. Stay low in your knees. Keep the ski's leading edge up—trailing edge down—by angling knees slightly away from the boat. Keep your rope arm bent slightly, so you can pull in and let out the handle, thereby making balance adjustments. Your free hand should be extended rearward for better balance.

HINTS: If the ski feels very slippery, slow the boat down a mile an hour at a time until it feels better. If you are catching an edge and falling forward, the ski is bogging; speed it up a bit.

TYLL ATTEMPT RATIO: 10 to 30 tries

Bounce slightly, release left hand, turn to left.

When ski reaches sideslide, keep leading edge up.

ONE-SKI FRONT-TO-BACK 180
60 POINTS

1. **Assume** a vertical crouch position. Ski directly behind the boat.
2. Bounce upward releasing left hand.
   a. Leading the turn with your head.
   b. Stay very low in the knees.
   c. Turn rather briskly.
3. Pull right hand, holding handle, toward right hip.
4. Grasp handle with both hands when in 180 position.
   a. Keep head up, looking at shoreline.
   b. Knees bent. Stay low.
   c. Arms bent; knuckles touching small of back.

NOTE: After your first successful one-eighty, stay in that position to see how long you can ride backward. After more tries, practice crossing the wake backward to get the "feel."

AL TYLL ATTEMPT RATIO: 4 to 10 tries

Assume vertical crouch, directly behind the boat.

Turn, pulling the handle in right hand toward hip.

Bounce up, release hand, stay low, turn briskly.

Grasp handle in both hands when in 180° position.

Ski backward in vertical crouch position, above.　　At up part of bounce, right hand lets go of handle.

ONE-SKI BACK-TO-FRONT 180

60 POINTS

1. **Ski backward** in vertical crouch position.
   a. Head up.
   b. Handle in close.
   c. Knees bent.
   d. Start bouncing slightly.
2. At the "up" part of a slight bounce:
   a. Right hand lets go of handle.
   b. Left hand keeps handle in close.
   c. Lead the turn with your head as if trying to see what's going on in the boat.
   d. Stay low, over your binders.
3. As 180 turn is almost completed:
   a. Left arm holds handle in close.
   b. Stay low in knees.
4. As soon as ski is in front position, grasp handle with both hands.

AL TYLL ATTEMPT RATIO: 5 to 10 tries

180 turn is almost completed; handle held close.

As soon as ski is in front position, use two hands.

ONE-SKI 360

90 POINTS

TO DO A THREE-SIXTY, JUST DON'T STOP IN THE ONE-EIGHTY POSITION. KEEP HANDLE IN CLOSE. KNEES BENT. HEAD ERECT. REMEMBER, DON'T HESITATE DURING THE TRICK.

TYLL ATTEMPT RATIO: 20 to 40 tries

46

Bounce up and down in toehold position for "feel."

At "up" start left turn by turning head to left.

TOEHOLD FRONT-TO-BACK OR "TOE BACK"

100 POINTS

Get a good Al Tyll type trick handle which snugs up on your foot. Crude straps are not recommended because they come off the foot too easily. First practice riding on one ski in toehold position. Cross the wakes in this position. Even try jumping the wakes in this position to get the "feel."

1. Bounce up and down in toehold position:
   a. With both knees bent.
   b. Body low.
   c. Both arms outward for balance.
2. At the "up" part of a bounce:
   a. Start turn to the left by turning head in that direction. Ski will follow.
   b. Keep body directly over the binder; quite erect.
3. As body turns, swing with arms also, and:
   a. Keep knees fairly bent.
   b. Stay erect over ski.
4. As ski reaches 180 position:
   a. Skier's weight is directly over binder.
   b. "Rope" leg is bent.
   c. Arms extended for balance.
   d. Head erect, but eyes on water.

HINTS: When you've reached this position, ride in it for as long as you can to get the feel. Even try crossing the wakes backward.

AL TYLL ATTEMPT RATIO: 5 to 20 tries

As ski reaches 180 position; weight over binder.

As body turns, swing arms; keep knees fairly bent.

Just before you bounce to front position, above.

Begin bounce by straightening ski leg, moving up.

TOEHOLD BACK-TO-FRONT OR "TOE-FRONT"

120 POINTS

1. **Assume** back toehold position. Just before you bounce to the front position:
   a. Get lower by bending both knees.
   b. Keep head very erect.
   c. Arms extended.
2. Begin your bounce by:
   a. Straightening ski leg, moving body upward and unweighting ski.
   b. Lead turn toward the right by turning head in that direction.
   c. Keep rope leg bent for better control.
3. Your head leads the turn all the way.
   a. Your ski turns to front position easily during bounce.
   b. Arms help balance and control turn.
   c. Eyes on water in front of you.
4. As turn is completed:
   a. Body settles into lower but still erect position.
   b. Hands outward keep balance.
   c. Head faces directly forward.
   d. Rope knee is relaxing, almost extended.

NOTE: Many skiers fall backward as this trick is almost completed. Reason: They are not erect enough with upper torso and head, and should bend their rope knee more. This trick should be done fairly briskly. If you do the trick too slowly, your ski can catch an edge.

TYLL ATTEMPT RATIO: 15 to 35 tries

Arms balance, ski turns to front easily in bounce.

Completed, body is erect, arms out for balance.

48

Assume vertical crouch position; hold rope low, then bounce smartly and begin to turn as ski clears rope.

TWO-SKI STEPOVER FRONT-TO-BACK OR "LINE BACK"

80 POINTS

1. **Ski directly** behind the boat; in the center of the wake.
   a. Assume vertical crouch position.
   b. Hold rope very low.
2. Bounce upward *smartly* and:
   a. Swing right ski up toward rope, both knees bent.
   b. Let go with left hand.
   c. Start shoving handle toward water.
3. a. Unweight left ski and begin to turn it 180 degrees as right ski begins to clear rope.
   b. With your body unweighted (in "up" bounce position) your left ski can easily make its turn on the water.
4. As stepover ski clears rope:
   a. Keep stepover knee bent.
   b. Keep "handle hand" low, arms straight. This will be quite a strain.
   c. Keep head erect, not facing water, but more toward horizon.
5. As stepover ski touches water:
   a. Keep left hand outward for balance.
   b. Keep head up. Do not face toward water any more than you have to.
   IMPORTANT: 1. A smart bounce is necessary.
   2. Hold rope very low.
   3. Weaker skiers may hold on with both hands during trick using the "baseball-bat" grip.

TYLL ATTEMPT RATIO: 10 to 25 tries

As stepover ski clears rope, keep rope arm straight.

As stepover ski touches water; balance with arm.

Ride backward, head up, skis about 16 in. apart.

Bounce and push left ski while lifting right ski.

TWO-SKI STEPOVER BACK-TO-FRONT OR "LINE FRONT"

70 POINTS

1. **Ride backward.**
   a. One hand between your legs holding handle.
   b. Head up.
   c. Skis about 16 inches apart.
2. Bounce smartly and:
   a. Push against water with left ski while lifting right ski over the rope by bending right knee.
   b. Turn or lead with your head as if looking toward boat.
3. As your right ski clears the rope:
   a. Unweight the left ski.
   b. Begin to turn it quickly toward the front position.
4. At the peak of the bounce, your body is almost straight.
   a. Head up, facing forward.
   b. Right hand still holding handle in close.
   c. Right (stepover) ski has cleared rope.
   d. Left ski is still turning toward front position.
5. As the right ski touches water:
   a. Assume vertical crouch position.
   b. Head up.
   c. Quickly grasp handle with both hands.

AL TYLL ATTEMPT RATIO: 5 to 15 tries

As ski clears rope, unweight left ski, begin turning to front; as right ski touches water, use both hands.

| Assume crouch, hold handle in vertical position. | Pull, both hands; let right go as handle passes. |

Bring right hand around back, pulling handle in close to side with left hand; grasp with right hand.

WRAPPING FOR THE WAKE 360 OR "HELICOPTER"

There are two ways to do this trick—"wrapped" or "hand-to-hand." On ordinary 360s on the water, we pass the handle from one hand to the other. This is called "hand-to-hand." The wake 360 can be done this way and many champs use this method. It requires very fast, deft, rope handling since wake 360 turns usually take less time than water turns.

Most beginners feel that if they wrap one arm partly around their back, and grasp the handle on the other side, they can perform the trick without passing the handle, making rope handling one less worry.

So, I'll do the trick both ways, and let you decide which way you're going to learn it. If you've had a history of fumbling the handle during practice sessions, you might better learn the "helicopter" wrapped. If you are a quick, deft, more nimble fellow or gal, I suggest you learn the trick hand-

to-hand, for in competition you'll save wrapping time during those precious seconds of a high pressure trick run.

WRAPPING FOR A CLOCK-WISE (TO THE RIGHT) HELICOPTER

1. **Assume** vertical crouch. Hold handle vertical, arms outstretched.
2. Pull in with both hands, letting go with right hand as handle nears body.
3. Bring right hand around your back, still pulling the handle in close to your side with the left hand.
4. Grasp the handle with your right hand. Its forearm should be against the small of your back.
5. Rest your left hand comfortably on the rope, forward of the handle.

SUGGESTION: Start the clockwise helicopter from the outside, off the left wake, landing in between the wakes.

AL TYLL ATTEMPT RATIO: 1 to 4 tries

Wrap in vertical crouch, drift toward wake; at crest, bounce and let go forward hand; head leads turn.

TWO-SKI WAKE 360 OR "HELICOPTER"

110 POINTS

For a counterclockwise "Helicopter" (to the left), wrap your left arm around you, and grasp the handle with your right hand. Although these pictures show me doing the trick from the center of the wakes out, beginners would find it easier to first ski outside the right wake, and execute the trick from the outside inward, off the right wake. In each case, you are skiing to the left, and turning in that direction.

1. Wrap, and assume vertical crouch:
   a. About 8 feet outside wake.
   b. Drift toward wake.
2. Reaching the crest of the wake:
   a. Bounce briskly, and let go with forward hand.
   b. Lead turn with head erect, spinning on a vertical axis.
3. In the air, at 180 degrees:
   a. Spin on a nice straight vertical axis.
   b. Head erect, but leading turn.
4. In the air, at 270 degrees:
   a. Keep handle in close.
   b. Your free arm swings around freely.
5. Landing.
   a. "Give" in the knees to lower your center of gravity.
   b. Grasp handle with both hands.

AL TYLL ATTEMPT RATIO: 5 to 30 tries

In the air at 270 degrees; free arm swings freely.

"Give" in knees on landing; grasp with both hands.

52

TWO-SKI WAKE 360 OR "HELICOPTER," HAND-TO-HAND

For a counterclockwise helicopter, ski about 8 feet outside the right wake.

1. Assume low vertical crouch position and drift toward the wake, handle in close.
2. Reaching the crest of the wake:
   a. Bounce high, straight up, turning quickly.
   b. Lead turn with your head.
   c. Pull handle in *very* close.
   d. Right hand lets go of handle and starts reaching around back.
3. In the air, at 180 degrees:
   a. Right hand keeps handle in very close to back.
   b. Left hand grasps handle.
   c. Body spins on vertical axis.
   d. Right hand lets go after passing handle to the left hand.
4. Landing.
   a. "Give in the knees" for more stability.
   b. Grasp handle with both hands.

TYLL ATTEMPT RATIO: 10 to 50 tries

Ski 8 ft. outside right wake, drift in, crouch.

At crest, bounce high, turn quickly, reach around.

Switch hands, keep turning, lead turn with head.

"Give" in knees on landing; grasp with both hands.

53

Ski in center of wakes, vertical crouch, stay low.

At crest, hop 6 or 8 inches, let go with left hand.

Spin quickly, aiming for exactly 180 degree turn.

Landing in back position, eyes on water, head up.

ONE-SKI WAKE FRONT-TO-BACK OR "WAKE 180"

80 POINTS

1. **Skiing** in the center of the wakes:
   a. Assume vertical crouch.
   b. Stay very low.
   c. Drift toward the left wake.
2. Reaching the crest of the wake:
   a. Hop briskly, simultaneously beginning turn.
   b. Let go with left hand.
   c. Turn on an axis leaning slightly away from the boat.
   d. Don't hop too high—just 6 or 8 inches.
   e. Keep handle in close.
3. In the air, at 90 degrees:
   a. Right hand brings handle close by your side, toward small of back.
   b. Spin quickly, trying to make it exactly 180 degrees.
   c. You can be watching the water, but keep your head up.
4. Landing in back position:
   a. Left hand grasps handle.
   b. Except for your natural lean away from the boat's pull, you should be rather erect, eyes watching water, but head up.
   c. Staying low in the knees will lessen chances of falling.

AL TYLL ATTEMPT RATIO: 5 to 25 tries

ONE-SKI WAKE BACK-TO-FRONT 180

80 POINTS

Assume vertical crouch in backward position, about 6 feet outside the wake, head up, handle held against the small of your back.
1. Drift toward the wake.
   a. Knees bent.
   b. Head up.
2. At the crest of the wake:
   a. Bounce.
   b. Let go of handle with left hand.
   c. Lead turn with head toward the right.
   d. Right hand keeps rope in close.
   e. Turn toward the front quickly when you're in the air.
3. Landing.
   a. Knees give as ski touches water.
   b. Left (free) hand swings around; should grasp handle quickly.
   c. Head is kept erect, looking forward.
   d. Right hand has succeeded in always keeping handle in close.
   Note: Don't cut back too hard toward wake; just drift.

AL TYLL ATTEMPT RATIO: 3 to 15 tries

Drift toward the wake, knees bent, head held up.

At crest, bounce, release left hand, turn quickly.

Right hand keeps handle close, left arm swings. On landing, grasp handle quickly with both hands.

Ski directly behind boat in center of the wake.

Drift to wake, bounce, swing right ski up to rope.

TWO-SKI WAKE STEPOVER— FRONT-TO-BACK OR "WAKE-LINE BACK"

110 POINTS

1. **Ski directly** behind the boat in the center of the wake.
   a. Assume vertical crouch position.
   b. Hold the rope low.
   c. Drift toward wake.
2. As you reach the crest of the wake:
   a. Bounce upward smartly.
   b. Swing right ski up toward rope.
   c. Let go with left hand.
   d. Right hand keeps handle low, toward water.
3. Left (bottom) ski lifts off wake.
   a. Turn it 180 degrees.
   b. Right (stepover ski) clears rope. Keep that knee bent.
   c. Head up.
   d. Left arm swings, controlling turn.
4. Stepover is nearly completed, as bottom ski touches water after 180 degree turn.
   a. Keep handle low, arm straight and rigid.
   b. Keep head erect, facing horizon.
5. Stepover ski touches water (completing trick both physically and validating it in competition).
   a. Keep left hand outward for balance.
   b. Keep your head up.
   c. Knees bent.

AL TYLL ATTEMPT RATIO: 5 to 25 tries

Keep knee bent as ski clears rope; ski touches water after 180° turn; left hand out for balance.

Assume stepover position 6 ft. outside the wake.

Drift to wake, bounce, lift ski toward the rope.

Bend knees, turn wake ski to front, complete turn.

As both skis touch water, "give" in knees a bit.

TWO-SKI WAKE STEPOVER— BACK-TO-FRONT OR "WAKE LINE FRONT"

110 POINTS

1. **Assume** stepover back position about 6 feet outside the wake.
   a. Hold handle low.
   b. Head facing horizon.
   c. Hold free hand outward and to the side for balance.
   d. Drift toward the wake.
2. Reaching the wake, bounce briskly, and:
   a. Bend stepover knee, swinging that ski over rope.
   b. Water foot and ski help the bounce by pushing off the wake.
3. "Wake" ski lifts into the air.
   a. It begins its turn to front position.
   b. Head leads turn.
   c. Knees are bent, upper torso swings upward to a vertical position.
4. As both skis touch water:
   a. "Give" in the knees to assure stability.
   b. Grasp handle with both hands.

AL TYLL ATTEMPT RATIO: 8 to 25 tries

Ride center of wake, toehold position, drift out.

At the wake crest, bounce, keep bend in rope knee.

Ski lifts off wake, turn ski quickly, stay erect.

Land backward, weight directly over your binder.

WAKE TOEHOLD FRONT-TO-BACK OR "TOE WAKE BACK"

150 POINTS

First practice jumping the wakes in front toehold position, to get the feel of "landing" off the wake while only your toes are "holding on."

1. Riding in the center of the wake, in toe-hold position, drift toward the wake.
   a. Both knees bent.
   b. Arms outward for balance.
2. At the crest of the wake, bounce.
   a. Straighten ski leg for lift.
   b. Keep arms outward to maintain good balance.
   c. Keep a bend in your rope knee.

d. Keep your upper torso and head over binder.
e. Lead head in the direction of your turn.
3. Ski lifts off the wake.
   a. Turn ski quickly.
   b. Stay erect over ski.
4. Land backward.
   a. Skier's weight is directly over binder.
   b. "Rope" leg is still bent.
   c. "Ski" leg gives (or bends) with landing.
   d. Head is erect, but eyes are on water.
   NOTE: Always keep rope knee bent; upper torso erect, to prevent falling away from the boat.

TYLL ATTEMPT RATIO: 10 to 50 tries

WAKE TOEHOLD BACK-TO-FRONT OR "WAKE TOE FRONT"

180 POINTS

1. **Assume** back toehold position 6 feet outside wake, and drift toward wake.
   a. Get low, by bending ski knee. Also bend rope knee.
   b. Keep head and upper torso erect.
   c. Arms extend outward for better balance.
2. At the crest of the wake, bounce.
   a. Straighten ski leg for lift, and quickly turn ski.
   b. Lead turn by looking toward boat.
   c. Keep rope leg bent.
3. Just before the ski touches water.
   a. Ski turns easily to front position.
   b. Body is vertical, directly over ski binder.
   c. Head erect, facing boat.
4. Landing.
   a. Ski knee bends to assume lower, surer, position.
   b. Hands outward keep balance.
   c. Rope knee relaxes, almost extended.

NOTE: Many skiers fall backward upon landing. Reason: Their upper torso is not erect enough. Bending rope knee gives you much more control. Also be sure to make the complete turn in the air. If your ski doesn't land heading perfectly forward, you'll either catch an edge, or slide out. Turn briskly once off the wake.

TYLL ATTEMPT RATIO: 30 to 100 tries

Assume back toehold position 6 ft. outside wake.

Drift in, bounce off wake crest, quickly turn ski.

Still in air, body vertical, ski turns to front

Landing: torso is erect, ski knee bends; balance.

ONE-SKI WAKE 360 (WRAPPED)

150 POINTS

Similar to the two-ski helicopter which has already been pictured, these front angle sequence pictures show a counterclockwise wake three-sixty on one ski.

1. Wrap.
   a. Ski 8 feet outside the wake.
   b. Assume vertical crouch.
   c. Drift toward wake.
2. Reaching the crest of the wake, BOUNCE!
3. Leaving the wake, begin turning in the air.
4. Turning in the air:
   a. Spin on a vertical axis.
   b. Rope hand keeps handle in close.
   c. Head is still leading turn.
5. Landing.
   a. Give in your knees.
   b. Grasp handle with both hands.

TYLL ATTEMPT RATIO: 10 to 50 tries

At 8 ft. outside wake, start wrap, drift to wake.

Completing wrap at crest of wake, bounce briskly. Retain right hand hold on rope for balance here.

Leaving wake crest, begin turning around in air.   Still turning in air, free right hand, pull rope.

Complete turn in air; land with ski facing frontward; "give" in your knees; grasp with both hands.

ONE-SKI STEPOVER FRONT-TO-BACK

120 POINTS

Ski directly behind the boat on one ski. Take rear foot out of back binder. Hold rope very low. Assume vertical crouch position.

1. Bounce upward smartly and:
   a. Swing right foot up toward rope.
   b. Keep both knees bent.
   c. Left hand lets go.
2. Unweight ski and begin to turn it as foot goes over rope.
   a. Hold handle low. Arm straight.
   b. Hold free arm out for better balance.
   c. Body is in unweighted position; ski can turn easily without catching an edge.
3. As stepover foot clears rope:
   a. Keep both knees bent.
   b. Keep handle arm straight and low.
   c. Free arm is making balance adjustments.
4. Stepover is completed.
   a. Don't let foot dig in the water. This will throw you. Just let toes touch. Must touch to make trick legal.
   b. Keep head up.
   c. Keep handle low.

TYLL ATTEMPT RATIO: 10 to 20 tries

Free rear foot, bounce, swing foot up to rope.

Unweight ski and begin to turn as foot goes over.

As foot clears rope, complete ski turn; handle arm is straight and low; let toes touch to complete.

Ride backward, stepover foot touching water; bounce, lift foot to rope; body straightens, foot clears.

ONE-SKI STEPOVER BACK-TO-FRONT

110 POINTS

1. **Riding backward** with one hand between your legs, holding handle as low as possible.
   a. Keep head up.
   b. Stepover foot is just touching water with toes.
2. Bounce up in the knees.
   a. Push against water with left (ski) leg while bending right knee and lifting right foot over rope.
   b. Turn head toward boat, but keep it up high.
3. Body straightens as "bounce" takes effect.
   a. Stepover foot clears rope.
   b. Left ski is unweighted and turning easily toward front position.
4. Stepover three-quarters complete.
   a. Ski turns to front position.
   b. Handle is held in close.
   c. Left hand is swinging around fast, toward handle.
   d. Head is facing forward toward boat, but looking at water.
5. As right foot touches water:
   a. Assume vertical crouch position for stability.
   b. Grasp handle with both hands.

AL TYLL ATTEMPT RATIO: 5 to 15 tries

Stepover three quarters complete; ski turns free.

As right foot touches water, grasp, both hands.

63

Ski directly behind wake, free right foot, drift to wake; at crest, bounce, swing foot over, turn ski.

ONE-SKI WAKE STEPOVER FRONT-TO-BACK

180 POINTS

1. **Ski directly** behind the boat in center of the wake.
   a. Assume vertical crouch.
   b. Hold the rope very low.
   c. Drift toward the wake.
   d. Stepover foot should be out of back binder and held opposite "ski" foot.
2. On the crest of the wake:
   a. Bounce upward smartly.
   b. Let go with left hand.
   c. Swing right foot up toward rope.
   d. Keep handle low.
3. Ski lifts into the air.
   a. Turn it 180 degrees.
   b. Stepover foot clears rope. Knee bent.
   c. Left hand swings out for balance.
   d. Keep head up.
4. Ski touches water after "180."
   a. Stepover foot clears rope.
   b. Left arm outward for balance.
   c. Keep upper torso and head up.
5. "Stepover" foot is carefully lowered to touch water.
   a. Both knees are bent.
   b. All of your weight is supported by "ski" foot.
   c. In competition, "stepover" foot must touch water to receive points for the trick.

TYLL ATTEMPT RATIO: 25 to 100 tries

Ski touches water after 180 as foot clears rope.

"Stepover" foot carefully lowered, touches water.

Take "line back" position outside wake, drift in.

Bounce at crest, swing foot over rope; ski in air.

ONE-SKI WAKE STEPOVER BACK-TO-FRONT OR "WAKE LINE FRONT"

160 POINTS

1. **Assume** "Line back" position:
   a. About 6 feet outside the wake.
   b. Handle held low.
   c. Free hand held to the side and outward for balance.
   d. Drift toward the wake.
2. At the crest of the wake, bounce briskly.
   a. Bend stepover knee, and swing that foot over rope.
   b. Hold head erect, turning it toward boat.
3. Swinging toward the "front" position:
   a. Ski lifts into the air turning quickly.
   b. Head leads the turn.
   c. Upper torso straightens.
4. Ski touches the water.
   a. Skier lands with all his weight on the ski.
   b. Free foot is kept away from water's surface to prevent tripping.
   c. Body is almost straight, but ski knee will give on impact.
   d. Quickly grasp handle with both hands.

TYLL ATTEMPT RATIO: 15 to 50 tries

Head leads the turn to front, ski turning quickly.

Land with weight on ski, foot does not touch water.

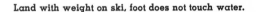

65

PREPARATION FOR THE TOEHOLD SIDESLIDE

This is one of the most difficult tricks. Competitors are required to "hold" this trick (in sideslide position) for two seconds. Believe me, those are two *LONG* seconds! When learning this trick you either "slide out" or "catch on edge" the first ten or twenty tries.

It is difficult because you only have one foot on the ski while it is sidesliding; no back foot as steadying leverage. SO—first learn to do a regular one-ski sideslide *WITHOUT THE BACK FOOT IN THE BINDER.*

1. With your foot loosely in the back binder, go into a one-ski sideslide.
   a. Stay low by bending the knees.
   b. Adjust the angle of the ski with your knees so that it is in a perfect sideslide.
2. Quickly, but smoothly, slip your rear foot out of its binder and try to hold sideslide position as long as possible. To save discouraging falls, as soon as you think you're falling, snap into the front position.

ADVICE: Practice this for three or four sessions until you can hold this one-foot one-ski sideslide for four or five seconds. Then, you can start working on the "T SS."

When you can do this—and smile—you're in!

With foot loosely in back binder—try sideslide.

Slip rear foot out; sideslide as long as possible.

Bounce in vertical toehold crouch position; at "up" of a bounce, unweight ski and snap into sideslide.

THAT TOUGHIE! THE TOEHOLD SIDESLIDE

250 POINTS

1. **Bounce** up and down in "toehold vertical crouch position."
   a. Both "rope" and "water" knee bent.
   b. Body low, right over the binder.
   c. Both arms semiextended for balance.
2. At the "up" part of a bounce:
   a. Unweight ski by snapping it out of its forward track into the sideslide.
   b. Keep both knees bent.
   c. Arms out—one to side, and one toward front, for balance.
3. Approaching "sideslide" position.
   a. Make sure to keep knees bent.
   b. Try to adjust your balance quickly to your new "coefficient of friction." It will feel slippery.
4. A good toehold sideslide, eyes on water or ski.
5. A tougher toehold sideslide—not watching the ski. Try it sometime.

NOTE: Practice, practice, and more practice, is the only secret to mastering this trick. If you catch an edge, angle the leading edge of the ski a bit more. If you "slide out" decrease this angle. Stay as low as possible to lower your center of gravity.

TYLL ATTEMPT RATIO: 50 to 250 tries

It's okay to keep eyes on ski and water with this.

The tough part—when expert—is to look away.

67

With ski knee bent, place right ankle behind left knee; hold pull with hand while putting on "handle."

TOEHOLD 360

220 POINTS

A difficult trick, but very perfectable by the average trick skier, with practice. Many competitors lose credit for the trick, because they hesitate (or stop) in the "180" position. A good trick handle is mandatory. Stay low, and turn vertically—right over your ski's binder.

1. For a clockwise toe three-sixty:
   a. With ski knee bent, place right ankle behind left knee.
   b. Place or fix the "U" part of the Trik Handle against the instep of the right foot.
   c. Keep some of the line's pull from the toehold foot by holding onto the line with your right hand.
2. Let go with both hands, and start turning.
   a. Straighten upper torso, leading to the right with your head.
   b. The rope will slowly begin to pull you around.
   c. Keep your right knee bent.
3. In the 180 position:
   a. Rope knee holds "bent" position, against the pull of the rope.
   b. Arms swing outward to give "fly-wheel action."
   c. Stay vertical, but knees should be bent.
4. Spin continues to 270 position.
   a. Rope knee begins to straighten under strain of rope. You're now beginning a simple toehold back to front.
   b. Head is still leading the turn.
5. As 360 is completed:
   a. Body settles into lower, but still erect position.
   b. Hands outward keep balance.
   c. Rope knee is relaxing, almost extended.

TYLL ATTEMPT RATIO: 50 to 100 tries

Let go with both hands and start turning on ski.   Swing arms for flywheel action in to pass 180°.

Rope knee begins to straighten at 270 position; head leads turn; at finish, settle, body still erect.

Drift from outside wake to crest, bounce smartly, release left hand and pull for fast turn in air.

In air at 180°—pull up skis by bending knees, pull in handle for fast turning, keep swing going.

TWO-SKI WAKE BACK-TO-BACK "HELICOPTER"

160 POINTS

Generally speaking this is like doing a wake front to back, and a back to front, in one motion, off one wake. AND, THAT'S WHAT MAKES IT A "#$%—&()*@"! For a clockwise wake back-to-back: Ski outside left wake, about 6 feet from it.

1. Assume vertical crouch position.
   a. Drift toward the wake, briskly.
   b. Keep handle in close; head high.
2. Reaching the crest of the wake:
   a. Bounce smartly.
   b. Begin a rapid turn.
3. In the air, in 90 degrees position:
   a. Lead turn with head.
   b. Body gains height as a result of good bounce.
4. In the air, in 180 degrees position:
   a. Pull your skis up by bending knees.
   b. Keep your turn going.
   c. Keep handle very, very close to your body.
5. Beginning the last 180 degrees:
   a. Grasp handle with left hand.
   b. Right hand lets go—keeps the "swing" going.
6. Landing.
   a. Left hand, keeps handle in very, very close.
   b. As skis touch water, grasp handle with your right hand (this is difficult), or, make an immediate positioning turn (toward the left) on the water without ever touching handle with right hand.

TYLL ATTEMPT RATIO: 50 to 150 tries

In full turn, grasp handle with left, right lets go.

Landing; handle is in close, both hands optional.

ONE-SKI WAKE BACK-TO-BACK "HELICOPTER" OR "WAKE BACK-BACK"

210 POINTS

A **healthy lift-off** and fast, deft, rope handling is essential for this wake trick.
1. Ski 8 feet outside the wake in backward vertical crouch.
   a. Keep handle in very close.
   b. Drift toward the wake briskly.
2. Reaching the crest of the wake:
   a. Bounce smartly, leading the turn with your head.
   b. Turn quickly.
3. In the air, in the 180 position:
   a. Left hand prepares to grasp handle.
   b. Bend the knees a bit, you'll pull the ski up higher.
4. In the air, in the 270 position:

a. Right hand lets go—keeps the "swing" (turn) going.
b. Left hand pulls handle in even closer.
c. Head still leads turn.
5. Landing.
   a. Left hand strains to keep handle in close.
   b. Skier keeps head up; knees bent.
   c. Grasp handle with both hands.*
   *ALTERNATIVE: It is very difficult to hold the landing position after a back-to-back trick. It is much easier to do a trick positioning turn back-to-front a moment or two after landing. Using this alternative, the right hand need not grasp the handle, but upon landing the skier would merely do a fast 180 to the left to again assume a frontward (and more stable recovery) position and actually get credit for the 180.

TYLL ATTEMPT RATIO: 70 to 300 tries

Ski 8 ft. outside wake in backward vertical crouch position; drift briskly toward wake, handle close.

Reaching crest of wake, bounce briskly for height, spin briskly for complete turn in mid-air as shown.

In the turn at the 180 position; pull knees up, switch hands as you swing around for back landing.

WAKE TOEHOLD THREE-SIXTY FRONT-TO-FRONT

300 POINTS

A very difficult trick. A good trick handle is necessary. Stay low and keep a good vertical spinning axis, right over your binder. Always do this trick from the outside of the wake inward—landing between the wakes.

1. Skiing 8 feet outside the left wake:
   a. With ski knee bent, place right ankle behind left knee.
   b. Place the "U" part of the Trik Handle against the instep of the right foot.
   c. Keep some of the rope's pull from the toehold foot by holding onto the rope with your right hand.
2. Reaching the crest of the wake:
   a. Let go with both hands and start turning with head.
   b. Bounce.
3. Rising off the wake.
   a. Rope knee remains bent against the rope's pull.
   b. Body, arms, and head lead the turn of the ski.
4. In the air, in 180 position:
   a. Ski spins very fast.
   b. Arms swing for a controlled turn.
5. Turn nears completion.
   a. Rope knee begins to straighten.
   b. Stay directly over binder.
6. Landing.
   a. Rope knee straightens under momentary tightening of any slack that may have been caused by the trick.
   b. "Ski" knee "gives" for smooth landing.

TYLL ATTEMPT RATIO: 50 to 500 tries

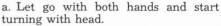

Attach "U" part of Trik Handle to right instep.

Ski outside left wake, drift to crest, bounce up.

Rising off wake, spin fast, body, arms and head all lead turn; aim ski for front landing position.

Rope knee straightens under momentary tightening of slack that may have been caused: ski knee gives.

Front approach; assume low vertical crouch, aim for center of ramp. See "Jumping" on pages 86 to 93.

RAMP TRICKS IN GENERAL

Ramp tricks are easy. Really! No kidding!

First ski straight over the jump on your trick skis at your usual trick speed, with the boat passing parallel to the right side of the ramp, and about five feet from it. If you go straight up the ramp, you'll land about five to eight feet outside the wake. If you wish to land inside the wakes, your driver should carefully pass very close by the side of the ramp, say, one foot away. You would plan your course diagonally up the ramp, approaching it in the center, but leaving the right hand corner.

Most trick skiers prefer to land outside the wakes. So do I. Tolerances of driver idiosyncrasies, judgment, boat speed, and rope lengths aren't quite so critical if you plan an outside-the-wake landing. Also, many drivers occasionally scrape the ramp sides. This situation isn't healthy.

You'll find that most ramps are much "faster" than the water; hence tricks seem very slippery at first. Trick skis just don't track up a waxed ramp, making proper balance and a spinning axis perpendicular to the ramp surface essential. Deft rope handling, a very low vertical crouch and a quick spin are also desirable for clean, neat ramp tricks. As a conditioner, practice some very fast 360s and 180s on the water while skiing outside the wake. Even at 16 miles per hour the skier is on the ramp less than one second.

RAMP FRONT-TO-BACK (RAMP 180)

90 POINTS

Tell your driver to drive 15 or 16 mph, five feet from the side of the ramp, and parallel to it. Ski outside the left wake.
1. Front approach.
   a. Assume low vertical crouch.
   b. Aim for center of ramp.
2. Skis touch ramp.
   a. Begin turn immediately.
   b. Keep head up.
   c. Keep handle in close.
3. On ramp 90° position:
   a. Pass the handle just below buttocks.
   b. Keep low in the knees, weight evenly distributed on each ski.
4. Approaching ramp 180 position:
   a. Grasp handle securely with both hands.
   b. Keep head up.
   c. Skis parallel, one foot apart.
5. Leaving the ramp in 180 position:
   a. Freeze in vertical crouch
   b. Ride off the ramp *without a pop, spring, or bounce.*
   c. Wait until your skis leave ramp before doing the air turn (next trick).

AL TYLL ATTEMPT RATIO: 1 to 10 tries
NOTE: For a ramp 360, merely spin faster on the ramp. To receive credit for this trick in a tournament, the whole turn must be completed on the ramp surface.

As skis hit ramp, start turn; release left hand, pass handle below buttocks, grasp with both hands.

Leaving ramp in 180 position; skis parallel, about one ft. apart; freeze; do not spring or bounce off. For a ramp 360, merely spin faster on the ramp; the whole turn must be completed on the ramp surface.

AIR BACK-TO-FRONT (FROM THE RAMP) OR "AIR FRONT"

120 POINTS

1. **Leaving ramp.**
   a. Do not bounce or pop.
   b. Don't start turning skis until they have cleared the ramp.
   c. Let go with left hand.
   d. Start leading turn with your head.
   e. Stay low.
2. In the air, in 90-degree position.
   a. Knees bent.
   b. Freeze in crouch position, but keep turning, toward front.
3. Air turn completed.
   a. Free arm swings around with turn.
   b. Skis are one foot apart for sure, solid landing.
4. Landing.
   a. Give in knees upon landing.
   b. Keep rope in close.
   c. Swinging arm should grasp handle quickly.
   d. Land five to ten feet outside the wake.

AL TYLL ATTEMPT RATIO: 1 to 10 tries

Leaving ramp—do not pop or bounce. Don't start turning until skis leave ramp; release left hand.

In air in 90-degree position; knees bent; freeze in crouch but keep turning, leading turn with head.

Air turn completed; skis one ft. apart, arm out.　　　"Give" in knees on landing; grasp, both hands.

AIR FRONT-TO-FRONT OR "AIR FRONT-FRONT"

210 POINTS

1. **Ski straight** up the ramp in very low crouch.
2. Leaving the lip of the ramp:
   a. Begin to turn.
   b. Lead with your head.
3. In the 180 position:
   a. Keep handle in close.
   b. Prepare to grasp handle with other (left hand).
4. Leaving the 180 position, left hand grasps handle.

5. In 270 position:
   a. Right hand has let go of handle; swings with body.
   b. Left hand attempts to keep handle in close.
6. The 360 is almost completed.
   a. Skis parallel.
   b. Body turn is nearly completed.
7. Landing.
   a. "Give" in the knees to absorb landing shock.
   b. Land five to ten feet outside the wake.
   c. Grasp handle quickly with both hands.

TYLL ATTEMPT RATIO: 10 to 50 tries

Ski straight up the ramp in a very low crouch.

Leaving lip of ramp, start turn, lead with head.

In 180 position, keep handle in close, prepare to grasp handle with other hand to keep swing going.

Leaving the 180 position; left hand grasps handle while continuing swing, leading turn with head.

Free right hand and spin, aim for straight-to-front landing; give in knees, grasp with both hands.

Approach ramp, at 30 feet begin your 180° turn.

Your 180 is almost complete just before touching.

RAMP-BACK APPROACH

40 POINTS

Very easy! But there seems to be a psychological barrier. Until you've had one try under your belt, you just know you're going to clobber that big water ski ramp, BACKWARD! Have no fear. After the first time, it's old stuff.

The secret is to delay your front-to-back until you barely have time to complete it before the ramp. Then the moment you feel your skis touch the ramp, begin a quick ramp 180 back to front. You'll probably do it on your second or third try.

1. Approach the ramp at 15 or 16 mph.
   a. Begin your 180 about 30 feet from the ramp.
   b. Plan to hit the ramp about middle.
2. Just before touching ramp:
   a. Your 180 is almost complete.
   b. Keep rope arm and handle in close.
   c. Keep one arm out for balance.
3. Skis touch ramp backward.
   a. Skis are about a foot apart.
   b. Knees bent.
   c. Head up.
   d. Wait for "solid feel" of ramp.

TYLL ATTEMPT RATIO: 5 to 15 tries

Touch ramp backward, skis about one ft. apart. Keep knees bent, head up, wait for solid feel of ramp.

RAMP BACK-TO-FRONT OR "RAMP FRONT"

90 POINTS

1. **Skier** hits ramp backward.
   a. Immediately begins to turn toward front position.
   b. Knees bent.
   c. Handle in close.
2. As turn progresses:
   a. Free arm accelerates turn.
   b. Skier still remains in low crouch.
   c. Head also leads turn.
3. Turn passes 90 degrees.
   a. Rope arm keeps handle very close.
   b. Head still leads turn.
   c. Skis remain about a foot apart for sure stance.
4. Turn is completed on ramp.
   a. Skis facing perfectly forward.
   b. Stay low, holding rope close.
   c. Skier is now ready to perform an air trick, or merely make a straight jump landing, whichever he desires.

TYLL ATTEMPT RATIO: 10 to 25 tries

As skis hit ramp, immediately start front turn.

Crouch, swing arm to spin, lead turn with head.

Turn continues; rope arm keeps handle in close.

Skis pointing perfectly forward at lip of ramp.

AIR FRONT-TO-BACK WITH A BACK LANDING OR "AIR BACK-BACK LANDING"

AIR FRONT-TO-BACK: 120 POINTS
BACK LANDING: 70 POINTS

The air front-to-back is a snap. But the back landing is a bit tricky. The secret is to "crush" or really settle in the knees when leaving the ramp. The lower you get, the more you seem to lessen the height of the jump. In other words, just the opposite of a long distance jumper! Your aim is not for distance but to land as softly as possible, but—backward!

1. Ski straight up the ramp in very low crouch.

2. Leaving the ramp, begin the air 180.
   a. Knees bent.
   b. Let go with left hand.
3. Stay in crouch position and turn.
4. As 180 nears completion:
   a. Stay in crouch position.
   b. Bring free (left hand) toward handle to grasp it.
   c. Keep head up.
5. Landing.
   a. Grasp handle with both hands.
   b. Give in knees upon landing.
   c. Keep head up.
   d. Pull handle in close to the small of your back.
   e. Keep skis about one foot apart. •

AL TYLL ATTEMPT RATIO: 5 to 20 tries

Ski straight up ramp in crouch; free left hand.

Begin air 180 by swinging arm, leading with head.

Freeze in crouch position, skis about one ft. apart, knees bent, both head and body leading turn.

Bring free hand around to grasp handle as shown.

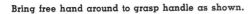

Landing: grasp handle with both hands, head up.

Jumping

How to jump safely in step-by-step instructions, photos and charts.

JUMPING SKIS

Closely resembling standard skis, most "jumpers" differ only in construction, weight and thickness. They range in length from 60″ for juniors, to 65-70″ for adults, and have one keel on each ski. The 6½″ width seems to be average; thickness between ⅝″ and 1″. Jumpers are usually constructed from laminated ash.

The manufacture of jumpers is tricky because of two essential desires: flexibility and durability. Since they take a heck of a beating, the skis must withstand great shocks and be generally unbreakable. "Beefing up" the ski would seem to take care of the breaking problem.

On the other hand, skiers like soft landings after flying off a 5-6′ ramp. Thicker skis are stiff and rigid—and land like a rock. The skier's heels, ankles, knees and vertebrae suffer under transmitted shock. The more flexible the ski, the less jarring the landing. Thinning the ski down makes it flexible—but fragile. A vicious circle.

Things are looking up, however. Manufacturers are starting to make better jumpers—and the prices are commensurate. (Anywhere from $50 to $100 per pair, without binders).

Before jumping, always make sure your jumpers have no screws or bolts protruding from the bottoms and that their keels are tight and smooth. If anything should catch on the ramp, it could send you spinning! And scratch the ramp surface as well.

Safety, of course, is *first*.

Jumping skis, right, are more flexible and durable.

Beginning jumper wears jump jacket or ski vest.

Use a 12 to 14 ft. jumping ramp, 4 to 5 ft. high.

Freeze in this position and let the boat pull you.

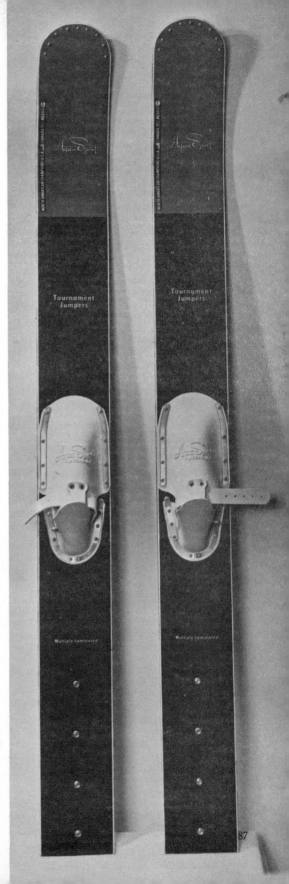

87

JUMPING FOR BEGINNERS
RAMP HEIGHT: 4 TO 5 FEET

Use a regulation 12- or 14-ft. waxed jumping ramp. Wear a good "jump jacket" or ski vest. Many skiers wear wet suits (1/8" neoprene) for protection. Tell boat driver you want 25 mph, and that he should drive 15 feet from the right side of the jump, and parallel to it. He should give you a long, straight approach.

1. First approach: In low vertical crouch position head for the left side of the jump.
2. When almost upon the ramp, freeze and allow the rope to pull you toward the boat. Keep skis about 8 to 12 inches apart.
3. Your path won't be straight up the ramp, but slightly diagonal toward the boat. Let your skis point in that direction. Remain basically rigid.
4. Keep this position in the air, too. Your weight should be directly over binders. Knees bent. Arms almost straight. Head erect, looking forward.
5. Your landing impact will be like jumping off the dining room table. Pull in slightly on the rope if there is slack, but there shouldn't be. "Give" slightly in the knees when you land, but don't bottom the fanny.

YOU *DID* IT? *YOU'RE A YUMPER!*

AL TYLL ATTEMPT RATIO: 1 to 7 tries

Beginners approach straight on to far ramp side.

When almost upon ramp, freeze in crouch, let the rope pull you toward the boat; skis 8-12 in. apart.

Your path won't be straight up the ramp, but will cut diagonally across toward the boat as shown here.

Retain rigid crouch in air, weight over binders.

Impact is slight; give in knees; pull for balance.

89

JUMPING: EXPERT— DOUBLE CUT METHOD

Latest Men's Record: Dennis Rahlves, 1964—158 ft.

Latest Women's Record: Co-held by Barbara Klack & Liz Allan—102 ft.

Most tournament jumpers want the tow boat to drive 40 feet from the side of the ramp. Before the boat enters the jump course they cut hard toward the opposite side of the boat and "hang" out there, waiting for the last possible moment to start a fast cut across both wakes toward the ramp. Naturally their speed is accelerated greatly over the boat speed (sometimes to 60 mph). The master "double-cutter," actually skis diagonally (right to left) up the ramp. This actually affords him a longer distance and time to travel on ramp surface, giving more time (a split second) to "pop" for more height—hence a longer jump. On the other hand, there is the ever-present danger of being "late"—that is to say, should the jumper not reach the ramp surface in time, he might possibly collide with ramp side, which could "smart," to say the least.

1. Jumper begins cut across both wakes, toward ramp.
   a. Skis about a foot apart, cutting hard.
   b. Skier very low in the knees.
   c. Gripping handle tightly and holding it in close.
2. Jumper nears the ramp.
   a. Cut until the last minute.
   b. Then plant weight equally on both skis.
3. Hit the ramp at lower right corner.
   a. Begin to rise, or "pop."
   b. Skis a foot apart, on the ramp.
4. At top of ramp, "pop" is at its maximum.
   a. Push against ramp with your skis.
   b. Pop upward and forward.
5. Freeze in good form in the air.
   a. Skis parallel.
   b. Legs straight.
   c. Bend forward at waist.
   d. One hand holds handle low. Free hand rests on thigh in good jumping style.
6. Skis touch.
   a. Body is directly over binders.
   b. Grasp handle with both hands.
   c. Stiffen knees for landing.
7. Landing.
   a. Bend forward at waist upon impact.
   b. Proof of a good double is landing way out to the left of the boat.
   c. Try to stay over your binders.

A GOOD JUMP!

AL TYLL ATTEMPT RATIO: 5 to 1000 jumps (depending upon jump distance) •

Expert jumper hangs far left, cuts across wakes.

Aiming for near corner of ramp, will cut across.

Cutting across wakes accelerates speed greatly; jumper starts to rise a bit upon hitting the ramp.

At top corner jumper pushes downward for "pop."   In air; free hand rests on thigh for good form.

"Pop" provides good distance; freeze in position.   Knees stiffen for landing; grasp with both hands.

Bend forward at waist upon impact, but stay over binders; land parallel to boat, far to the left.

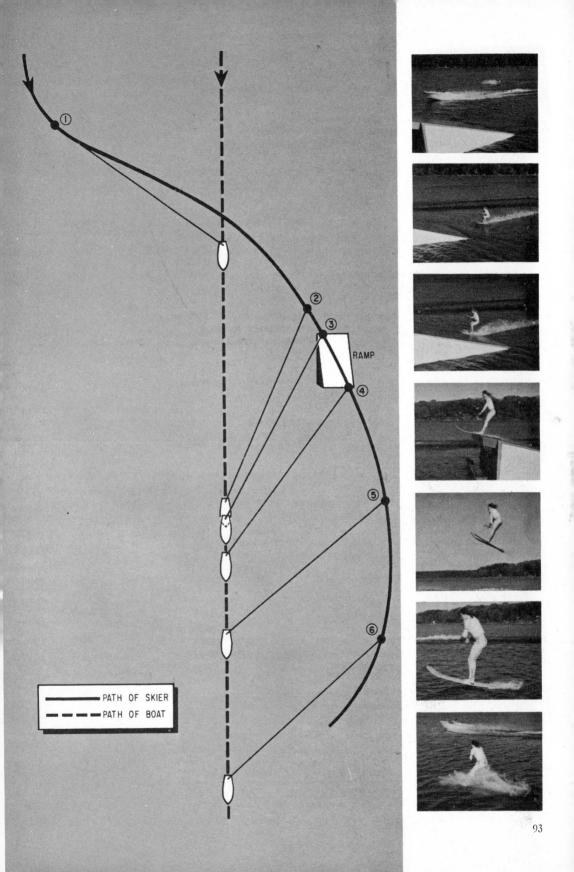

PATH OF SKIER

PATH OF BOAT

RAMP

① ② ③ ④ ⑤ ⑥

Barefooting

Here is a trick that is thrilling to both spectator and skier alike.

BAREFOOT "SKIING"

There's something about barefooting on water that's unparalleled in feeling of accomplishment and skier satisfaction. To be towed behind a speeding boat over a mirror-like surface, held up by only the surface of your heels against the water, never ceases to be thrilling to spectator and skier alike. The best way to learn to "barefoot" is to get out on the lake early some morning when it is glassy-calm, with the following "ingredients."

1. A boat that can pull a skier at least 36 mph.
2. A competent driver and observer.
3. A long stretch of glassy-calm water.
4. A good jump jacket, or other similar life preserver.
5. A 75-foot line.

6. The "Kick-Off" Ski: (in order of preference)
   a A "Freeboard" (ski with the binder removed so that he merely places his foot on the ski).

   or

   b. A regular straight ski with heel unit removed.

   or

   c. A regular ski or slalom ski with the binder adjusted very loose, so that it can be stepped out of quickly, without hindrance.

If you have average-sized feet for your weight and size, your speed will be around 34 mph. If your feet are larger than normal, 32 or 33 may do. If they are small for your size, barefooting will be more difficult for you—and you must have 36 mph plus.

The most important thing to remember

The stepoff! Moment of truth! When the barefoot feels like it's carrying half your weight: GO!

is the "SITTING IN THE CHAIR" position. Always remember that this is the proper position just before "step-off." Although many master the "step-off" right away, it usually takes a couple tries so be prepared for some uncomfortable, unexpected spills. If you feel yourself going, tuck quickly to avoid a hard body slam into the water at 35 mph.

ALL RIGHT. HIT IT!

If you're a right-foot-forward skier, you must naturally kick the ski off your right foot. Your best place to try barefooting is about eight feet outside the right wake. (There is turbulence directly behind the boat, so don't learn there) I'm "left-footed" so in the pictures, I'm outside the left wake.

1. SKIING AT 36 MPH

a. Get ready to dig in right foot.

b. Ski binder is adjusted wide open—very loose.

c. About eight feet outside the wake.

2. ASSUME "SITTING IN THE CHAIR" POSITION

a. Dig free foot (heel first), into the water about 18" from ski, and a bit forward of other foot.

b. Arms hold handle in "baseball-bat" fashion, half bent.

3. THE STEPOFF—(MOMENT OF TRUTH)

a. When the barefoot feels like it's carrying more than half your weight, quickly slip other foot out of binder and step heel-first onto the water.

b. Step either outward or inward—as you please, but lean backward a bit more during the step-off. This way you'll avoid uncomfortable forward spills. They smart!

4. BAREFOOTING—THE FIRST MOMENT OR TWO

a. Remain in "CHAIR SITTING" position, arms bent.

b. Lean well against the boat's pull, or you'll catch a toe and wham!

5. BAREFOOTING EASILY

a. Straighten arms, and back, and even knees a bit to get more comfortable, but don't get too brave right away. And, watch where you're going.

As of February, 1965, the barefoot time record was again set by Don Thompson of Lee's Summit, Missouri, whose best new record was 33 minutes, 3.2 seconds. The American Water Ski Association has initiated a separate barefoot club reserved for water skiers who "have skied continuously for at least one minute on their bare feet before an official observer." Rules for barefoot ratings may be obtained from American Water Ski Association Headquarters, Winter Haven, Florida. There are many unique ways of barefooting.

Using one ski, dig in heel of free foot, lift ski then kick it off quickly and ride on both heels.

Straighten arms and back a bit as you ride along.

JUMP-OUT: Ride along on two skis and jump out of both binders simultaneously landing on your bare feet—and ride away that way.

BEACH START: Sit down on a nice sandy beach (no pebbles) about 30 feet from the water's edge, with your feet pointing toward the water. As soon as the line tightens, the driver guns the boat, full throttle. You get dragged along the sand legs straight and hit the water about 15 to 20 mph—but, of course, the boat keeps on accelerating. At first you ride along on your thighs, surrounded by spray and water, but you hang on for dear life and when the boat hits 32 or faster, you bend your knees, dropping your heels into the water, and stand up. Not many do this barefoot start.

DEEP WATER BAREFOOT START: Lean back and sink in the water feet pointing toward the boat, handle held tightly against your thighs. As the boat accelerates, keep your back arched until you have surfaced and are riding along on your thighs. At 32 mph or faster, dig in your heels and stand up.

ONE FOOT BAREFOOT: Simply pick up one foot, but add at least 2-4 mph to your boat speed.

Prearrange a head nod to pick up 2 to 4 mph boat speed—then try this: barefooting on one foot only!

"JUMP-OUT" BAREFOOT

1. Ride along on two skis, at barefoot speed.
2. Jump up and out of your skis.
3. Bring your feet down, and in front of you, heels first.
4. As full impact of your weight comes down on your heels, you may tend to "fanny dunk." (It is better to do this than not to have your weight backward enough.)
5. Straighten a bit toward "sitting in the chair" position.
6. A unique way of ending your run—the front flip. Simply throw the handle, and tuck forward, tightly, like a tumbler. •

Ride along on two skis at barefoot speed for you.

When all is well and road is clear—jump up and out of both skis at once by bending knees as shown.

Bring feet down and in front of you, heels first.

As weight comes down on heels, fanny may dunk.

Straighten up toward "sitting-in-chair" position.

Unique way to end run is to release handle; tuck.

Competition

Some facts regarding an eventual aim of all those who water ski well.

AMERICAN WATER SKI ASSOCIATION

A nonprofit corporation organized under the laws of the State of New Jersey, AWSA is dedicated to the development and enjoyment of the sport of water skiing as a primary means of wholesome family recreation.

It serves as the governing body for the organized sport of water skiing, and its 13 national committees are engaged in specialized studies aimed at broadening participation in the sport as well as improvements in sanctioned competition.

Membership in AWSA is available at $5.00 per year; Family Memberships: $10.00. All memberships include a sub-scription to THE WATER SKIER, the official AWSA publication, including the YEARBOOK edition.

Encouraging water ski clubs, AWSA furnishes detailed information on club organization and manuals of suggested activities, including ski shows, community instruction, safety programs, publicity and promotion. Other aids and materials distributed by AWSA include national rating system, summer camp program and ratings, novice rules and booklets on every form of water skiing.

For complete details and information write:
AMERICAN WATER SKI ASSOCIATION
7th St. & Avenue G. Southwest
Winter Haven, Florida. •

AWSA REGULATIONS

DIVISIONS OF COMPETITORS, ACCORDING TO AGE:

DIVISION	AGE LIMIT	BOAT SPEED FOR JUMPING
Men	17 - 34	35 MPH
Women	17 - 29	28 MPH
Sr. Men	35 & over	28 MPH
Sr. Women	30 & over	28 MPH
Boys	13 - 16	28 MPH
Girls	13 - 16	28 MPH
Jr. Boys	12 & under	26 MPH
Jr. Girls	12 & under	26 MPH

ACCURATE SLALOM SPEEDS:

The speed at which the boat must pass through a 315 yard slalom course can be easily measured by timing with a stop watch from one end gate to the other. The actual times are as follows:

MPH	ACTUAL TIME (seconds)	MPH	ACTUAL TIME (seconds)
22	29.3	32	20.1
24	26.8	34	19.0
26	24.8	35	18.4
28	23.0	36	17.9
30	21.5	38	16.95

OFFICIAL TRICKS & THEIR POINT VALUES

Description	2 skis	1 ski
WATER SURFACE TURNS		
180° FB	30	60
180° BF	30	60
Basic 360°	40	90
Each additional 180°	10	20
Reverse 360°	40	100
Stepover 180° FB	80	120
Stepover 180° BF	70	110
Toehold 180° FB		100
Toehold 180° BF		120
Toehold 360° FF		220
Reverse toehold 360° FF		220
Toehold 360° BB		250
Reverse Toehold 360° BB		250
Sideslide	20	70
Toehold sideslide		250
Reverse toehold sideslide		275
WAKE JUMP TURNS		
180° FB	50	80
180° BF	50	80
360° FF	110	150
Reverse 360° FF	110	150
360° BB	160	210
Reverse 360° BB	160	210
540°	210	280
720°	260	320
Stepover 180° FB	110	180
Stepover 180° BF	110	160
Toehold 180° FB		150

Description	2 skis	1 ski
WAKE JUMP TURNS		
Toehold 180° BF		180
Toehold 360° FF		300
Reverse toehold 360° FF		300
Toehold 360° BB		330
Reverse toehold 360° BB		330
Somersault	280	350
MISCELLANEOUS WATER TRICKS		
Back swan		40
Back swan recovery		60
Deep water back start		80

RAMP TRICKS	On Ramp 2 skis	On Ramp 1 ski	In Mid-Air 2 skis	In Mid-Air 1 ski
180° turn	90	150		
Each addl. 180°	40	100		
Back landing, add	70	140		
Back app., add	40	90		
180° turn			120	180
Each addl. 180°			90	130
Back landing, add			70	140
Back app., add			40	90
90° turn SS ldg.	250	380	230	350
Back jump	170	290		
Straight jump		140		
Jump—both feet				
On ski thruout	240			
Somersault			430	570

Surfing

An introduction to surfing plus excellent comment on riding technique.

SURFING BEGAN when the early Polynesians modified their long twin-hulled canoes and one-man dugouts into shallower slabs on which they could stand up and actually ride the waves. With a short period out for puritanical "progress," the sport of surfing has been dominant in Hawaii—the paradise the Polynesians discovered thousands of miles to the north. The waves were huge, the sun was hot—and the ride was long. It was only a matter of time before the beach boys and the fiberglass set would take over. Like now.

Surfing, then, has come a long space across time and water—but the sport has remained remarkably unchanged. Gone, of course, are the square-tailed redwood planks and the solid giant Koa wood Olos, the lighter, stronger, more streamlined and more maneuverable modern boards having taken their place. The idea, however, is still to paddle out over (or through) the breaker line without falling off your board, wait for a likely looking wave—and ride it in.

The beginning surfer should be aware that, while he can walk into a sporting goods or department store and buy a good ready-made or "pop-out" board for anywhere from $75 to $125, he can probably get a custom-made board for only slightly more—say from $100 to $150.00. The beginner should look for stability and buoyancy—graduating to a smaller and more maneuverable board later. Resale, then, is important—another reason for investing in a better board at first. If you can sell—they can sell—which means you might ask around and see if there are any good buys before parting with your cash. Here is a chart with suggested dimensions for the beginner. . .

YOUR WEIGHT	BOARD LENGTH	THICKNESS AND WIDTH
80 lbs.	8'	2¾ x 21"
100 lbs.	8'9"	2¾ x 21½"
125 lbs.	9'	3 x 22"
150 lbs.	9'4"	3 x 22"
175 lbs.	9'8"	3½ x 23"
200 lbs.	10'2"	4 x 23½"

There are heavier, thicker boards for chunkier surfers; shorter boards for wake surfing (the new inland water sport—behind a boat) and long, thick tandem boards for carrying your girl friend on your shoulders. Check your cash and make your choice.

While some balsa boards are available, the majority are of polyurethane foam covered with fiberglass. Kits, too, are marketed, in both precast and preshaped blanks. You do some of the work and save some of the money. Some guys get as much fun out of building their boards as they do using them. Depending on the surf, of course.

The following information was supplied to us by Abe Schuster Fiberglass, 6211 Telegraph Ave., Oakland, California. He warned us not to alter a word of it—and we haven't. *The Editor*

Oahu is Mecca, but Southern California has more surfers; sport is spreading fast all over the world.
FPG photos

103

Surfing Tips

By Doug Elliot of the
United States Surfing Association

READY TO WAX

Now that you have your expensive and beautiful new board, it's time to get it wet and wax up. The most popular wax used is plain grocery store sealing paraffin. With the paraffin rubbed over the face of board, you have less chance of slipping off the slick polyester surface.

Physical condition and swimming ability are extremely important in surfing. For the moment we will assume you can swim and are in fair physical condition.

PADDLING

Paddling is the first and most important step in surfing. The only way one can get out to surf a wave is by paddling. There are no rope tows or chair lifts such as in skiing. This is like walking up the hill to ski down and is just as exhausting. Much practice must be devoted to learning the various ways to paddle to become proficient enough to "get outside" easily and with a minimum of effort.

The most common method of paddling is in a prone position. This is with the body flat on the top of the board, balanced so the nose stays about two or three inches out of the water. If the nose is lower, it may drag down into the water and if too high, could cause too much drag by the tail being too low in the water. The feet remain together on the board, toes outstretched. The arms are used to stroke or pull the board through and over the water. The stroke is much the same as the butterfly stroke in swimming, with both arms working simultaneously.

For some surfers this is the only way to paddle and catch waves, while with others it is the most tiring method. The next most popular method is by kneeling. Again the body and weight is positioned to keep the nose two or three inches out of the water.

GETTING OUTSIDE

Paddling out would be a small problem if there weren't waves to go through or over. The beginner must learn to conquer the difficulties in getting out through the breakers line without falling off his board. There are several ways to do this and there are a few points to keep in mind.

One must have momentum or be pad-

To "get outside" paddle fast in prone position; five ft. from wave, move forward and grip rails.

Once outside breakers, wait for the one you want. Easiest waves to catch are those which have broken.

dling fairly fast to get through or over the wall of water in a wave. Waves can be moving toward the beach at a speed of from 10 to 20 miles per hour. If you're sitting still in the water, you can be pushed toward the shore very easily. The idea is to shove through with your momentum. The safest and best way on a small broken wave is to paddle in a prone position until you are about five feet from the wave. At this point, move your body forward and grab both rails or sides of the board with a firm grip. Moving slightly forward puts more weight on the nose which keeps it down. If you are too far back, the wave may knock the nose up into the air and a backward somersault could result.

On smaller waves the knee paddlers can make it through by applying the same principles of weight forward and momentum. Naturally this is tricky due to the tippiness of the surfboards; consequently, this method takes a lot of practice.

SITTING THROUGH A WAVE

While waiting for the right wave, the surfer often doesn't bother to point through waves if they are small. He merely sits back on the board raising the board's nose two, or two and one half feet out of the water, while facing toward shore. The wave will pass, moving the surfer only a few feet. That is unless the wave is larger than expected. In this case, the board and surfer may be upset or taken toward shore.

To go through or under larger waves, a different method is employed. Momentum is still important. Just before you meet the wave, take a deep breath and roll over with the board on top of you. Lock your legs and arms around the board with your head still under the water. The wave will then roll over you and the buoyancy of the board and your body will cause both to rise to the surface. This is about the only safe way to get through or under larger waves.

In the old days with the heavier wood and/or balsa boards, it was possible to shove them through and dive under the wave, meeting the board on the other side, the weight and forward motion causing the surfboard to go through the wave alone.

Standing up is the last step in surfing the "soup." From position of hands and knees, rise up sideways.

CATCHING THE EASY ONES

When beginning, the easiest waves to catch are those which have broken. The resulting foam is called "soup." Practice in riding the "soup" can prepare you for riding unbroken waves. Paddle out into position. Depending on how far out the wave breaks would determine how far from shore to go. Usually one third to one half the way out is adequate. Keep your board pointed out to sea and directly into the waves until you are rested and ready. When the wave or soup coming in is to your liking, swing around and point toward shore. Lie down in prone position and adjust weight so the nose of the board is 12 inches out of the water. This high nose is necessary to keep it from catching or "pearling" when the wave picks you up. Pearling means to dig the nose of the board into the water, stopping your forward progress. The board can submerge to the bottom and cause some frustration and embarrassment. While catching the wave in the prone position, it's all right to have your legs off the back of the board to some extent. Paddle hard just before the wave reaches you. As it hits your back, grab the rails and hang on. Being too far back results in too much drag and will cause you to drop back and out of the wave. The larger the wave, the more force it has to pick you and your board up and shove it toward shore.

Let's assume you've caught the soup after a few tries. The next thing to learn is how to guide or turn a board. This is done merely by leaning one way or the other. The curved edge and bottom of the board cuts the water and causes the turning motion in the direction it is tilted. After a few runs, making turns while prone, it's time to try it on your hands and knees. The same principles apply and balance is still essential. Try this many times until you feel you have the knack and confidence.

STANDING UP

Standing up is merely the last step in surfing the soup. From the position on your hands and knees, rise to a standing position, sideways. Keep one foot about 18 inches ahead of the other, the rear foot crossways to the length of the board. The forward foot should be similarly situated, but pointed about 15 degrees or six inches toward the nose of the board.

Balancing and shifting weight are done from this position. If the nose comes up, lean forward on the front foot. If the nose goes down, lean back on the rear foot.

Some top surfers say the only way to learn is to jump up immediately rather than to kneel first. There is some merit to what they say, but for the novice it's very difficult to maintain balance when standing up quickly. Again, practice many times before attempting the next step.

RIDING UNBROKEN WAVES

The ultimate in surfing is to catch and ride as fast as possible across the face of an unbroken wave. The larger the better for some surfers. To catch the unbroken waves is rather difficult for the beginner. To be in the right position is a problem even for the expert. The correct position in this sense is the best spot to be in to catch the wave. This is where the ridge of the wave "peaks" to its highest point and causes the steepest slope in front of it. The steeper the slope (to a point) the easier it is to catch the wave. Only experience

teaches one to watch for the peaking areas and position.

MINUS A SKEG

Now imagine a surfboard on a steep mountain side. The board would start to slide down the mountain after being released. This principle of gravity, sliding, is exactly what moves the board down the face. Paddling to catch up with the speed of the wave and to get the board sliding down the face is your job. After you have caught the wave, the sliding action takes over and your job is then to control the slide.

The first problem encountered is that the surfboard can slide faster than the wave. If headed straight down, it could continue until the nose penetrates the "level" water and "pearls," often going straight to the bottom.

To overcome possible pearling, immediately after getting started one must move way back on the board, keeping the nose up. On very steep and fast waves this is not enough. Turning is essential to keep from pearling where speed is involved. The turn can be started by paddling and catching the wave on the angle rather than straight off (or straight in). Another way

Inland "wake surfing" is a way out for those who cannot get close to good breakers. It's not bad.

Florida Cypress Gardens photos

To overcome possible "pearling" one must move back on board, keeping nose up; turning is one way out.

to turn is to lean on the edge of the board until it comes around, pointed in the proper direction. It is easier to turn when kneeling until one can learn standing up after much practice. Most beginners miss the wave because they quit paddling too soon or are too far back on the board. Flat waves tempt the novice and wasted effort results. Again, experience helps judge when and where to start paddling.

STOPPING

While cut-outs aren't exactly a method of stopping, they do fall in this category to keep you from going any farther than you want to go on a given wave.

The best and easiest method for the novice to stop is by dropping into the water alongside the board, gripping across to the opposite side rail. This acts as a sea anchor would, and can be done before or after you catch the wave. The larger the wave, the more one has to grip.

STOPPING—STEPPING BACK

Near the end of the ride when your speed has decreased, stepping back on the tail of the board can stop you. The action forces the tail down into the water to act as a brake while the nose sticks up two or three feet out of the water.

Grabbing a rail and turning into the wave while shooting across the face can also bring you up in the back of the wave. This is often done when the wave starts to close out; "closing out" meaning the whole face of the wave has broken and become soup.

SITTING AND STOPPING

Just sitting down on top of the board with the feet extended down into the water can give a braking action. This can only be used in some instances and is not too desirable when headed down the face of a fast and steep wave. •

Wake "surfing" is term used for riding surfboard off the sides of large boat wakes as shown here.

Real surfers scoff—but the ride is longer and you don't have to wait around for nature's whim.

We had towers and booms for cameras—even a director! When he finished telling us off—I dunked him.

How to Ride a Book

Bantam Lake looked like Hollywood while we were taking the pictures.

This is a picture of Chris taking a picture of me while I ride behind the boat taking a picture of her.

Neighbors Eddie Digimas, 14, and Dom Ruccio, 13, combed their hair and drove for me after school.

On weekends, Howie and June Mitchell, our training buddies, drove while Chris took the photos.

Special angle shots had Chris playing high wire artist! She did everything but shoot underwater.

When we had company, we'd have a camera party. How to entertain without interrupting work.

Sometimes, of course, the company would entertain us! Try skiing while laughing. Dangerous!

Mostly, though, it was serious business. Here Chris is towed on our boom rig for neat side shot.